Named + Known

*Uncovering the Identities of
Women Who Plant Churches*

Edited by Heidy Tandy

Cover design by Grace Johnson. info@gracejohnsondesign.com

Interior design by Lena Roberson. lenadroberson@gmail.com

ISBN: 9781794638105

CONTENTS

PROLOGUE

There's No Better Time to Be a Woman

Dori Gorman

There are some questions you don't forget, no matter how forgettable they may be. There wasn't anything special about it. It was one you'd hear in a small group or on a bad first date—one of those cheesy things you ask to break the ice. Although the question itself wasn't much, the conversation that followed was more. "If you could be alive in any generation, any decade of history, when would you want to be born?" Think about it. What would you say?

Without hesitating, she looked at him and answered, "Right now. There's no better time to be a woman."[1] He tilted his head to the side, looking a bit surprised while giving serious thought to her response. He hadn't even

---

1   This conversation happened in a restaurant in Chicago and came from the perspectives of two people who were born in the United States of America. The title of the prologue is also from this perspective. For the sake of brevity, I chose to leave off, "There's no better time to be a woman in the United States" or other descriptors that could have easily been added on. This is important to point out since women from other places or with different backgrounds than mine may find it discouraging or even insulting to think that there is not better time to be a woman. With this in mind, I hope my words can be an encouragement to all women. There is still a long way to go, and many women have faced obstacles that I have never encountered due to my privilege. At the same time, I would like to think that most of us have come a long way from the days of Mary Magdalene.

thought of his gender when asking the question. He didn't have to think about it, but she did. It made him thoughtful; it made her reflective, and together they sought to better understand each other.

Imagine what it would be like to ask this same question to Mary Magdalene, Joanna, Susanna, and the other women who often traveled with Jesus during his lifetime. Of course it's challenging to put ourselves fully in their shoes without letting our modern Nikes get in the way, but what if they responded the same way? Without hesitating, I can hear them say, "Right now. There's no better time than right now to be a woman." Of course, they were walking and talking with the Son of God—who wouldn't want to be born during those decades? From their unique perspectives, however, this wasn't just revolutionary because he was the Christ. It was revolutionary because the long-awaited Messiah had a place for women unlike anything they had experienced before.

How did Jesus value women? He empowered them. He allowed women to travel with him[2] at a time when women were encouraged not to leave their homes. One Jewish writer of this time, Philo, recognized only two types of women: the ladies (astai) and the harlots (pornai). Ladies, according to Philo, live mostly in seclusion with full devotion given to home, husband, and children. Harlots, in contrast, appear in public, join religious cults, practice magic, or engage in sexual misconduct.[3] While Philo's culture as well as his fear created these oppressive categories, Jesus made a place for the supposed "harlots" and the "ladies"—seeing them, above all else, as humans. This was rare and subversive. By including women in his travels, Jesus empowered them beyond their station and their category, and he gave them a place with him.

As they travelled, Jesus gave a woman a seat at his feet while he was teaching. To our modern ears this doesn't sound like much, but Mary's one small step of kneeling was actually a giant leap for Jesus' disciples. One first-century teacher, Rabbi Eliezer, said, "Rather should the word of the Torah be burned

---

2   Luke 8:1-3.

3   "The Perception of Women in the Writing of Philo of Alexandria" by Dorothy Isabel Sly, McMaster University (September 1987), 149.

than entrusted to a woman." While this phrase has been debated for modern interpretation, there's no arguing that this was taken quite literally among Rabbi Eliezer's first century listeners. In contrast, Jesus elevated Mary by entrusting her with his teaching, giving her a place alongside her male contemporaries who would also sit at the feet of their Rabbi. To top it off, Jesus praised Mary for doing "what is better" and refused to allow her learning "to be taken away from her."[4]

Some of the women who were impacted by Jesus remain nameless—not to him but to us. Undoubtedly they were named and known by Jesus. But the male authors who recount their stories, perhaps due to their "uncleanliness," only refer to them as "a woman caught in the act of adultery,"[5] "a woman with an issue of blood,"[6] and "a Samaritan woman."[7] While they share anonymity, each woman is given a unique calling. One woman is commanded by Jesus to "Go and sin no more."[8] One is comforted to "Go in peace and be freed from your suffering."[9] One goes back into town and begins to tell everyone, "He told me everything I ever did," and with those words many believe in Jesus because of her testimony.[10] With a unique calling from Jesus—a command, a comfort, a commissioning—each woman also receives the universal love of Jesus, a love that elevates them like nothing before.

Jesus then calls another group of women, not only to give testimony but also to serve as witnesses. At a time when the testimony of a woman did not count in a court of law, the resurrected Jesus first appears to Mary Magdalene.[11] In another Gospel account, a group of women are with Mary Magdalene at the empty tomb, including Joanna, Mary the mother of James, and other women.[12] Together they are commissioned to tell the good news that Jesus

---

4 Luke 10:38-42.

5 John 8:1-11.

6 Matthew 9:20–22, Mark 5:25–34, Luke 8:43–48.

7 John 4.

8 John 8:11.

9 Mark 5:34.

10 John 4:39.

11 John 20:11-18.

12 Luke 24:10.

is alive. Not surprisingly, they aren't believed at first. Initially, several male disciples needed to see it for themselves. But, despite the doubts of men, one can't help but notice Jesus' choice of who to appear to first.

How did Jesus love women? Women traveled with Jesus, learned from Jesus, received unique callings by Jesus, and gave witness to Jesus. In light of this, I can imagine hearing Mary Magdalene, Joanna, Susanna, and other women from the Bible saying, "There's no better time to be a woman." When I eavesdrop on Jesus in the Bible, I hear a clear message—Jesus loves women and empowers them alongside of their male partners. As if that wasn't enough, when I eavesdrop on other conversations today, I hear the same desire.

I didn't intend to overhear their conversation. I wasn't raised to make a habit of eavesdropping. But that's what I found myself doing seven years ago in a Chicago coffee shop. My husband and I had moved to Chicago to join what God was already doing in Edgewater, a north side neighborhood that is one of the most diverse zip codes in the city. In our first year as church planters, we spent most of our time listening to our community. With an Assets Based Community Development approach, we knew that listening is a vital first step to starting a church that is in the neighborhood, with the neighborhood, and for the neighborhood. As the "father of modern medicine" Sir William Oslo once said, "Listen to your patient; he is telling you the diagnosis." But this time he wasn't telling me the diagnosis. She was. Three shes to be exact. Three women were having a conversation about the kind of place they were looking for if they were ever going to be a part of a local church. And that's when I began to listen, intentionally eavesdropping to hear what they would say.

More than anything else, they wanted a place where women were valued at all levels of leadership. They wanted a place where all voices were respected and intentionally given a seat at the table. One of the women said she'd probably never go to church. But if she did, that kind of church—one with women serving alongside of men as partners—would be the only one she would consider. I couldn't take it anymore. I broke the social code and finally spoke up. Apologizing for eavesdropping, I introduced myself and began to tell them about our church plant. I mentioned the radical love that Jesus has for all people, but specifically women, and invited them to check out a church that seeks to demonstrate that same love.

Jesus loves women and has a place for us in the church. Many of our non-Christian neighbors will only consider this kind of church. And Stadia is one of the best organizations for planting this kind of church. Stadia partners with leaders to plant churches for all people. Stadia partners with church planters: women and men who travel together, learn together, receive unique callings together, and are commissioned together to share the good news of Jesus' resurrection. There's no better time to be a woman.

How have I seen Stadia empower women? In 2015 NewStory Church became a Stadia church plant, and that partnership has given me a place that I never had before. From the very beginning I was valued as an equal to my husband—neither above nor below him, but with him. I have received coaching and been asked to coach others as well as assess future church planters through Stadia's Church Planting Assessment Centers. I have been given opportunities to teach workshops, preach sermons, write a book,[13] and partner with this book along with some other amazing Stadia women.

As someone who has been in ministry for twenty years, Stadia has given me more support and empowerment than any other ministry I have partnered with and served. Stadia values women so much that they have a specific ministry, Bloom, devoted solely to maximizing the role of women in church planting. Here's one story of how Bloom has helped Betsy Spring discover how her calling to church planting actually fulfills the passion of Jesus that was instilled by her father.

There has never been a question in my mind about whether my father loved me; after all, I was a daddy's girl. I was very close to my dad; I would even go as far as saying I believed in myself because my dad believed in me. My father was a very spiritual man, my pastor, and the person who introduced me to Jesus. My dad, however, did not believe in women preachers. This has been a lifelong battle for me as I am a woman who believes that I've been called to preach. Bloom has been essential to my life as I navigate the path of reassurance that my father loved me and would be proud of me, even though I am a woman who preaches. As a female leader in a church, this community

---

13   Gorman, Dori with Sara McGue, Anonymous: Naming the God of Esther and the Women Who Plant Churches, CreateSpace Independent Publishing Platform (April 7, 2017).

provides a safe place for women like me to learn, share, and continue to lead when the very foundation of their life is shaken by their calling and conviction to share the gospel. Though my father is deceased, his spirit and voice live in my heart. Unfortunately, Satan tries to use that voice to condemn me. Bloom is helping me to embrace the spirit of the father who loved me, while following the call of the Father who sent me.

Bloom truly values every possible level of leadership for women. Some church planting women are called to focus on their home and their families, supporting their husband as he plants and pastors the church. Other church planting women aren't married, co-pastor with their husbands, or have husbands who aren't pastors, and they are the ones called to plant a new church. Some church planting women work on staff at a church plant. Other church planting women have jobs in their community where they live as missionaries through their careers. Church planting women, like our male colleagues, come in all shapes and sizes. And Bloom strives to provide a seat at the table for all of us, just like Jesus did.

Many things can stand in the way of women in church planting. The voices of family members, friends, home churches, and traditions can often keep women trapped between two loyalties—the call of Jesus and the convictions of others. Bloom comes alongside of every woman in the midst of this cacophony and encourages us to be still to hear the voice of our Image-Maker, the One who names us and knows us. Jesus travelled with women, healed women, taught women, cried with women, challenged women, commissioned women, and so much more.

Bottom line: Jesus loved women. So does Stadia. And Stadia doesn't just want you to hear that message via eavesdropping. They want to shout it from the rooftops. What is it exactly that Stadia wants to say? Let's stop starting churches with one hand tied. Jesus has a purpose for all people. That purpose is not bound by gender but is empowered by the gifting of the Holy Spirit upon all individuals. May women pastor next to men for the sake of the gospel. May women serve next to men for the sake of the world. May women plant churches with men for the glory of God. Jesus demonstrates it, the world demands it, and Stadia is doing it. There's no better time to be a woman.

INTRODUCTION

For Such A Time As This

Heidy Tandy

In May of 2018, Stadia's Bloom Staff team sat on a porch overlooking Lake Erie, brainstorming about the next season in our ministry to help women maximize their roles in starting churches. We were prepared: notebooks in hand, laptops out, a flipboard with possible theme ideas for 2019, and a box of assorted chocolates that we managed to finish during our three-day planning session. It was go time.

We were, however, stuck.

We knew the subject, the area we wanted to cover: identity. This topic kept coming up as we talked to women in church planting. Who am I as a woman? As a church planter? As a pastor? As a leader? Am I even a leader? What am I good at? What is MY identity? For the purposes of this book, we are defining identity as the distinguishing characteristics or personality of an individual, one's sense of self. But we still were not set on a theme.

There's a scene on the television show The Office where Andy Bernard (played by Ed Helms) gets stuck too. He is trying to think of the jingle for the Kit Kat candy bar. He sings, and feel free to hum the tune along in your head, "Give me a break. Give me a break. Break me off a piece of that ____ ____ ____." And he gets stuck. He cannot remember the rest of the advertisement. He fills it in with everything from "Fancy Feast" to "Chrysler Car" to "Applesauce." At one moment you think he's going to get it--as a viewer you're yelling at the TV because you know the answer, but he just cannot find it. Like many scenes on this legendary program, the awkward tension was excruciating.

Have you ever had a time where you felt like you couldn't find "it"? You knew you were close, but you couldn't nail down an answer, a title, a creative burst to effectively get the job done? That's how it felt on the porch that day. We knew we were close to nailing down what we felt was an important theme over the next year for Bloom, but we weren't there yet.

We got a lot done during that planning retreat, but we left without a theme. We knew it would eventually come together but wanted to take more time to prayerfully consider what the theme for the year should be.

A couple of months went by, and we still hadn't nailed something down. More conversations. More brainstorming lists. More confirmation about this topic but no theme. I sent a text message out to some leaders in Bloom to help get our creative juices flowing: "Ladies, what are some words that you think of when you think of identity? Help us out!" Did they ever! We finished the day with an even longer list of words to add to our original brainstorm. We were so close!

Fixed.

Unmoved.

Anchored.

Flourish.

Engaged.

Worthy.

Thriving.

Empowered.

Two words were then mentioned in the text thread that began to weave together. First was the word named. In 2017, Dori Gorman and Sarah McGue wrote the fourth Bloom book, Anonymous. It seemed like a seamless transition to move from being anonymous to being named. Anonymous was an incredible book of stories from women based around the characters in the story of Esther. In this ancient text, God weaves throughout the story, even though his name is not mentioned one time. The shining verse from this text in Esther is when Mordecai says to her, "...And who knows but that you have come to your royal position for such a time as this?"[1]

Culturally, it feels as if we are in a "for such a time as this" moment. It is definitely an interesting time to be alive. And for women in church planting leadership, there seems to especially be some God-ordained opportunities. With the #metoo, #churchtoo, and #timesup movements, as well as the public failings of men in power both inside and outside the church, our identity as women and what we will be known for is in prominent focus. We are seeing women in the church being given a louder voice and more opportunities for leadership advancement now more than ever before. Previously held ideas about what a woman in ministry looks like are being shattered.

And then another word that kept coming up was known. At birth we are identified. Named. Told what our name will be for the rest of our lives. Our personalities, our preferences, and our potential, to the rest of the world, is unknown at this point. Yet our Jesus knows us. He knows who we are as women. As church planters. As pastors. As leaders. As sisters. From the beginning, we are known.

Then for the rest of this life, we are given the opportunity to develop a deeply and firmly held sense of ourselves: our identity. This secure identity is found in Christ alone, even through seasons where we don't know who we are,

---

1   Esther 4:14.

where our identity is mistaken, or where we face the unexpected. We also have the gift of knowing Christ and the power of what he did for us.

Named + Known means being confident in our calling and secure in our identity.

Named + Known means quitting the comparison game that says one type of woman leader is greater than or less than another.

Named + Known means that we show up to our churches and communities with a strong sense of who we are, not who we aren't.

Named + Known means we learn, we listen, and we celebrate our own uniqueness as women of God.

In these pages, you will read the stories of church planting women. This book is divided into four sections, with four women in each section sharing a story (or stories) that reflect their experiences as it relates to identity.

The first section is unknown identity. The women in this section share stories of learning new things about themselves; leaning in to who they really are in deeply formative seasons of life.

The second section is mistaken identity. Frequently in this world of church planting we can get sideways: maybe we think we are supposed to be like someone else or someone else has expectations of us that are not rooted in reality. The church planters in these pages share their stories of comparison, correction, and crisis.

The third section is unexpected identity. Church planting can be unpredictable. Our journeys don't always look like we planned--whether that's in our churches or our families (or both!). These women share surprises along the way and the impact of these unexpected moments.

The fourth and final section is secure identity. The women in these chapters share the areas where they have found freedom and contentment and how they got there. None of us is ever finished, right? But we can claim victory and should acknowledge times when the Lord has done a good work in us!

So within these stories of church planting women, you'll hear from women who have planted churches in the last year, fifteen years ago, and everywhere in between. These women lead in diverse ways: as pastors, on staff at churches, in the marketplace, at home with kids, as single women, on the east coast, on the west coast, and across the United States. Each woman is uniquely and purposefully made for her own story: for such a time as this.

Named + Known

SECTION 1

UNKNOWN IDENTITY

Named + Known

I Wanted to Be a Marine Biologist

Heidy Tandy

I wanted to be a marine biologist.

In seventh grade at Francis Hazen Junior High School in Minerva, Ohio, I was invited to participate in a job shadow program where I would get to visit a career mentor in a specific field and follow him or her around for the day. I didn't know how to use a curling iron, let alone know what I wanted to be when I grew up, so I honestly wasn't that interested in the opportunity.

Then I found out you could go to Sea World.

I heard through a big-time eighth grader that if you said that you wanted to be a marine biologist, you would get to go to Sea World during the school day and get a behind-the-scenes tour with a Sea World staff person. All I had to do was say that I wanted to be a marine biologist for my job, and I would get to go meet a real-life marine biologist at Sea World.

It made sense to me: I liked swimming, I really liked whales, and I was totally game to go to Sea World during the school day instead of actual school. So

I filled out the paper and wrote in my best seventh grade girl handwriting: I would like to be a marine biologist.

The year was 1997, and there was still a Sea World in the most illogical place ever: the ever-so-tropical Cleveland, Ohio. So on a cold April day, job shadow program imposter Heidy, another student who actually wanted to be a marine biologist, and our guidance counselor began the ninety minute journey to explore the vocation of marine biology.

Turns out, in April it's cold for the wildlife at Sea World in Cleveland, Ohio. Also, marine zoological parks are not nearly as fun in the dreary spring as they are in the summer. I was pretty disappointed—and I still had to write a paper about what I learned from my experience as a junior marine biologist. Spoiler alert: I am not a marine biologist. Just because I shadowed a marine biologist twenty years ago does not qualify me to lead the dolphin show.

Sometimes I feel even less qualified to be a woman in ministry, let alone a church planter. Prior to our church planting adventure, my husband Josh was on staff for almost eight years at two different churches. We got married in February of 2016--fresh out of college, twenty-two year old babies, ready to change the world through youth ministry. We moved to a parsonage (free house!) that we loved, painting the walls in the kitchen chalky blue and the bathroom a deep red that I still regret. I think everyone in his or her twenties has to have some sort of poor painting color choice as a rite of passage into adulthood.

What we lacked in experience, we made up for in energy and passion. And desserts. At First Christian Church in Moweaqua, Illinois, I learned to make desserts. We were thrilled to be building relationships with families, investing in a church, and opening up our home to students multiple nights a week. I tried out banana pudding, chocolate cake, and snickerdoodle recipes on skinny high school students with high metabolisms. (It was also in this season where I gained fifteen pounds due to said banana pudding, chocolate cake, and snickerdoodles.)

Josh had felt a calling to vocational ministry at eighteen years old at a CIY conference, and I wholeheartedly supported and affirmed that calling. I was all in for a life of work particularly in the midwest American church. I told him in college that I was fine eating ramen noodles and canned pineapple for the rest of my life if cash flow was low (that seems a bit dramatic now and high in carbohydrates and sodium).

But what about me? It sounds selfish, but it was simply an honest question that I asked a lot during this stage of life. I had friends who were teaching and having an incredible impact in the classroom, working at well known non-profit organizations, and traveling the world. I was working at Starbucks with a plan to go to graduate school (insert millennial joke here). As passionate as I was about helping students find and follow Jesus and partnering with Josh in ministry, ultimately my name wasn't on the paycheck. I was confident that I had a unique calling and purpose, but I still felt like just Josh's wife in the church.

One of the realities of getting married young is that we grew up together. While no one is ever finished growing and developing, the learning curve in the early twenties is steep. I put incredible pressure on myself to learn like Josh, reading the same books, listening to the same sermons, and talking about the same deep theological brewings. While none of these things are inherently wrong, I realized a few years into our ministry journey that (shocker) Josh and I aren't the same! The unique ways that we connect with the Lord are just that: unique. For me, the first step in learning who I was as an independent adult included a lot more about figuring out who I wasn't versus who I was.

As cliché as it may sound, the work that God did in my life in those first almost four years of ministry life is still impacting my story today. I began to learn in those beginning years that I really connect with God mostly through music and being by myself outside. I learned I am comfortable leading a room--and not just in icebreakers, games, or announcements. I learned I can read a room, sensing dynamics when people feel left out or misunderstood. I learned that my favorite students were the ones who weren't the coolest or most popular but the ones who were just a little bit weird, just like me. I learned that even though we loved opening our home, my top priority was my marriage and my family, even though at the time it only included my husband and our puppy.

All of these areas where I learned about myself continue to be building blocks for who I am as a woman in church planting. When we got started, I had no idea what I was doing, but I was a whole lot more confident in my calling and my identity than I was at twenty-two. In our first few years of pre-launch and planting, the learning curve was steep (if you're in pre-launch right now you know exactly what I am talking about!), but the season was incredibly formative. I often say that church planting is the adventure of our lifetime up to this point and that I love it, but unfortunately this sentiment about church planting being an adventure does not adequately convey the internal work that goes with planting a church.

To fully live in our Christ-given identity, we must do the hard work of learning what we aren't. The pieces in this section are stories of unknown identity. Therefore, the women who are sharing were asked to explore times in their lives that were deeply formative when they learned something new about themselves. This "something new" was more than a title, leadership responsibility, or role. It was a knowing.

Being named and known often begins with being named but not knowing exactly who you are. One of my favorite authors, Brené Brown, challenges me even with the taglines of her books. The tagline of The Gifts of Imperfection reads, "Let go of who you think you're supposed to be; embrace who you are."[1] This embracing is a process--a process that I am grateful for as a woman in church planting. I am also so very glad I am not a marine biologist.

---

1   Brown, Brené. The Gifts of Imperfection: Let Go of Who You Think You're Supposed to Be and Embrace Who You Are. Center City, Minn.: Hazelden, 2010.

Beauty in the Chaos

Kasey Jane

As I write, I'm sitting here on the beach in Florida. We live in Central Illinois, but my whole extended family has come to Miramar Beach for the week to celebrate my parents' 50th wedding anniversary. I've been trying to write this chapter for weeks, but I can't help but wonder if I needed to be here in this moment to gather my thoughts. I come from a big family with five siblings. This means there are fourteen adults and twenty-seven children (and one on the way) gathered together in one beach house. Being here is quite the experience.

With forty-one people under one roof, it's absolute chaos. The noise level is at an all-time high. The family dynamics are in full swing. You can just imagine what it's like bringing seven families back together with seven different ways of doing things. We've got too many cooks in the kitchen. The amount of food it takes each day to feed everyone is astounding. It's been raining four days straight, and the sun isn't due to shine until the day after we leave. There are nine bedrooms in this huge house, but there's nowhere to hide.

What better way to ponder your identity than going back to your roots with the people who helped shape you—good and bad? Of course we've had tension, screaming kids, sibling rivalry, accidents, feelings getting hurt, and a whole lot of opinions. But the truth is, these are my people. I love my family, and this week has created a lifetime of memories. There's no place I'd rather be than right here in the middle of this beautiful chaos.

Ironically, being here has helped me reflect on my experience in church planting. We planted Connect Church five years ago in my hometown of Washington, Illinois. I'm not sure anything could have truly prepared me for all that we would face. Many times in the beginning I felt like I was holding on for dear life. I remember saying to my husband, Dave, "Don't forgot to take me along with you." You would think that being raised in a crazy big family where organized chaos abounds would prepare me for a lifestyle of church planting and the many unknowns up ahead. I'm not sure that it did.

Let's back up a little bit for just a moment. Dave and I met through a school of ministry called ACE Teams. He's a Brit and moved to the U.S. to pioneer this ministry school for college-aged students. Dave is the life of the party and always has a story to tell. He's the first born with only one sister. He loves adventure and can't sit still. He's the most secure person I know and is forever an optimist. He lives for experiences and has a serious case of FOMO (fear of missing out). Needless to say, I was certain this new adventure of church planting was God's plan for him, and he would shine.

On the other hand, I'm an introvert through and through, and I thrive in a small group setting or one-on-one conversations. I'm a homebody who gets refueled with alone time. I love order, lists, and a clean house. I dislike change and surprises. (I'm a snooper and have been known to unwrap presents then rewrap them!) I fall in the middle of my five siblings (shout out to middles—my heart is big for you!), and I'm also an identical twin which adds a whole other dimension. I'm realistic, logical, and overthink most decisions. I knew one hundred percent that church planting was our next step in ministry, but to say I was hesitant is probably an understatement.

We had been in ministry for over fifteen years, including running ACE Teams and being involved in two other church plants (not knowing one day we would lead one). Over the years, I had found my niche raising my babies and hanging out behind the scenes where my introverted personality could call the shots. I considered my pastor's wife role to be the best possible support to my husband; I was mom to Benn, Will, and Emma with a side of leading small groups and mentoring. I was comfortable and just fine with the roles I played. Then church planting came on the scene and wrecked my little cozy life of ministry. I had always said I never wanted to be a pastor's wife—be careful of what you don't wish for.

Trying to find my new normal and role as the lead pastor's wife proved to be the most challenging during our first couple of years. Like staying in this nine-bedroom house, it felt like I had nowhere to hide. During launch phase I went into protective mom mode trying to keep my kids from turning into "those pastor's kids." I was also concerned our marriage would suffer. I went overboard worrying about family time and date nights. I would make sure Dave wouldn't give too many church chores to our kids, and I constantly monitored our calendar. I instantly felt new pressures and dwelled often on how I couldn't live up to the standards I created in my mind of a lead pastor's wife.

I also thought assessment would be the end of me. I'd love to say it was right up my alley, but mostly, it was my worst nightmare. Of course, Dave loved it. What's not to love about being thrown into a lead pastor's role, speaking in front of people, being intently watched, psychologists asking extremely personal questions, and not knowing what's coming around the next corner? I felt as though I was thrown into his element—where he was shining, and I was sinking. Assessment was intense and seemed to create such inner turmoil in me. I just prayed I could hold it together and not ruin my husband's chances of planting a church. There's one phrase that has always stuck with me, though, from those short few days at assessment: "We want you to realize you can do more than you think you're capable of." At the time, I was annoyed, and it wasn't what I wanted to hear. I was just relieved we were approved for church planting despite my chipper, sunny perspective (insert sarcastic tone here) while we were there. But little did I know all that our young church would soon endure.

Two months after launching Connect, a tornado tore through our town on a Sunday morning while we were in church. It wiped out one thousand homes, including much of our neighborhood. Our home only had minimal damage so we were able to postpone our repairs until the dust settled, literally. The need was great and the devastation greater. This became a year-long recovery process. During that same year, Dave and I had been walking alongside Connect families in desperate crises: marriages were severely suffering, a family lost their newborn baby girl, and a twenty-six-year-old member of our church lost her battle with cancer. These tragedies consumed me. To add to these circumstances, we were also dealing with some unhealthy staff dynamics that became a constant focus, and I was struggling with a family relationship causing an uproar inside me. Everything became too much.

While trying to control it all, I put so much undue pressure on myself. I let perfectionism creep in setting me up for failure, which led to me backing away and not wanting to commit to anything. I worried a lot about events and minor things. Small tasks overwhelmed me. I began to deal with anxiety, which I had never experienced before. It was at this point I began to question who I even was anymore. Despite trying to keep everything under control, I was feeling the opposite. My biggest mistake was not taking care of myself and thinking I was alone.

I began counselling to unpack what on earth led me to feeling so out of control and overwhelmed. In the months to follow, the stress triggered some pretty significant health issues leading to a diagnosis of a painful autoimmune disease. To say I was angry and heartbroken was an understatement. Here I was trying to serve God and follow his calling into something I would have never chosen, but pain and anxiety seemed to be my new normal. Shortly after my diagnosis, I still made it to the yearly Bloom retreat. It was there where God spoke so clearly to my heart that I was his, he loved me, and I was enough. It was as if everything else no longer mattered, and my core was transformed.

I had grown accustomed to letting everyone else know how much God loved and cared for them, but I had completely lost sight of this truth for myself. Feelings screamed loud, and truth felt like a faint whisper. I've learned to quiet myself to hear his whispers and let his truth guide me. My identity comes directly from Christ, then everything flows out of that understanding. To me, unknown identity are two words that are polar opposite. Identity is being known. Identity is knowing who you are in Christ. Until then, it is only undiscovered identity.

Looking back, I can see how God had his hand on my life and put the most amazing people in my path during such an incredibly hard season. The day after the tornado, our Stadia project manager came to help strategize cleanup efforts. Debbie Jones, the Senior Director of Bloom at Stadia, also called to see what she could do to help. Throughout all of the hardships and health issues, I had women in Bloom to reach out to for support and prayer. This was vital for me moving forward. I will forever be thankful for Stadia and specifically Bloom for the amazing support in my journey. God used our church planting experience to grow me in ways I so desperately needed and led me to explore deep in my soul. He doesn't leave us stuck, and our valleys don't define us. He is right there with us every step and taking care of our little families along the way.

Church planting has brought so much true joy to our family. My kids are now eighteen, sixteen, and eleven and I truly believe God used this experience to seal their faith. Our marriage has grown and will continue to do so. My autoimmune disease is now in remission, and these good days remind me to not take my health for granted. God has shown up for me in so many ways. The countless stories of life change God has done in our community also amaze me. I wish I had another chapter to share with you all the wins and incredible things God has done in and through us. Church planting is hard but a gift God used to make me more into the person he created me to be. There's no place I'd rather be than right here in the middle of this beautiful chaos.

The Perfect Woman

Vanessa Bush

At the same time my husband and I planted in Albuquerque, New Mexico, some acquaintances of ours were planting their church in another area of the country. The wife in the relationship was someone I had admired from afar for some time. She was gregarious and kind. Her love for Jesus was put on display with her life. She was quite the fashionista and always looked so put together. Do not, I repeat do not, compare her Instagram feed to mine. Her family had adorable matching outfits all the time, whereas I feel accomplished if my kids are clothed in something relatively clean. She was a fantastic leader. She organized ministries with one pinky, I'm pretty sure. She did all the things I felt like I should have been able to do effortlessly.

As our church planting journey continued, I met more women in church planting sprinkled all across the country who all seemed so wonderfully gifted. In my mind, they were all so very type-A and just really had their acts together. They were executing, check-listing, and administrating all the things. They could lead teams and put together committees with one hand tied behind their backs. Many of them were even co-pastoring with their husbands.

When I stood next to these other women in ministry (or rather placed them next to myself in my imagination), my insecurities flashed red in my mind's eye.

I remember vividly a conversation my husband and I had about a year into our church planting journey. This was about the time the excitement had worn off. I had strong-armed myself into doing so many duties I was not gifted for, hence I was getting weary. I actually apologized to him for my personality. I revealed to him that I thought he had married the wrong person because I could not do the spreadsheets and the administrative processes and the org charts. And if I looked at any church management software for one second longer, I would probably die.

My husband looked me in the eyes and said, "You are exactly the right person for me."

He showed me qualities I hadn't been able to see as gifts. I moved thousands of miles from my home and saw every step as a grand adventure. I embraced New Mexico enthusiastically and was committed to understanding my place. It was my frontier that I'd been divinely sent to. I optimistically thought every person I encountered was probably the next member of our new church. I planned their baptism services before we had even had a conversation. I was always in the mood for a party. And I didn't mind when he brought people home for dinner last minute. My rose-colored glasses were so thick that it didn't even occur to me that our church might not make it. I had an unwavering faith that God was in control. If I were the type of person who needed all my ducks in row, the uncertainty and highs and lows of our church planting journey would have made me lose my feathers.

We've all heard comparison is the thief of joy. But did you know it also robs you of seeing truth and fulfilling your purpose?

God has given me a fingerprint that is unlike anyone else's because he has a purpose for me that no one else can fulfill. My husband, my church, and my city need me, not someone else. They certainly do not need the make-believe, perfect, cookie-cutter women in church planting I had created in my head and was exhaustedly trying to become. And the reason why I was exhausted was because, of course, those women don't even exist.

After realizing my foolishness, I committed myself to truly understanding who God has created me to be. If there is a personality test, I've taken it. I'm an Enneagram 9, Myers Briggs ENFP, an i on the DISC, and I know all my strengths in the StrengthsFinders. I've realized I have a spiritual gift of discernment and am striving toward growing that gift.

Of course, we say God doesn't make mistakes when he creates people and when he calls people to do certain things (like church planting, for instance). But if you're anything like me, when you're in the weeds of life, that truth can be hard to ingest. We have to be prepared for the lies of the enemy that tell us we are not the person we should be or that our personality is unfit for the job.

Imagine a church that tried to replicate another church in a different area with a different culture with people who have different mindsets. It would never work out. The same is true of people. Trying to become who we think we ought to be rather than who we were definitely made to be will result in burnout and frustration.

We must learn who we are—who the Creator has created. When the One who spoke star dust into existence exhaled into our lungs, what parts of his nature did he want us to exhibit with our one and only life? It's pretty easy to confuse who we are with what we do, even if what we do is something as noble as church planting. God has created something beautiful in you, and you, not someone else, are exactly who has been sent to your church plant and to your community. You can have faith that if God has sent you to do the job, you're the right person for it.

Abundantly More

Dimetra Barrios

About to graduate, I needed something. Fear started to choke me like a noose around my neck. I felt the air leaving me, my breath becoming uneasy. My anxiety was high. I spent all this money to go to school and all this time studying just to be confused about who I was and what God wanted for my life.

I was in my third year as an undergrad at Liberty University. Seven years of my young adulthood were spent being a stay-at-home mom. As if I didn't have enough on my plate, I added the responsibility of becoming a student to make the most of my time. I was getting a degree in a field that would allow me to help people in the church. I knew God wanted me to do that much, or did I? Did I even hear him correctly? Did he even speak to me?

On this day of my life, I just didn't know. I didn't know my calling. I didn't know my life's plan. I barely knew what I looked like in the mirror. Everything was a blur. My eyes were failing me. That's when I lost it. I remember slamming the door behind me loud enough for my husband to hear. I wanted him to know I was unhappy. I convinced myself that he didn't care and couldn't fix my problem. I convinced myself that no one could for that matter, not even God.

Now what? Both the kids were old enough to go to school. Soon I would have to do something, but how could I do something if I didn't know who I was or even what I wanted? I'm not just a stay-at-home mom anymore. I'm not just a wife. Soon I wouldn't even be a student. Who am I? Those were the thoughts in my head as I slammed the door powerfully, only to cry with my face buried in my insecurities. It was official: I didn't know who I was apart from the labels I gave myself.

I was so angry, so lost, so desperate. My thoughts kept racing. You learned about this Dimetra. What are you going to do about it? Coming up short, I did what I remembered David doing in Scripture. I got mad at God. That's right—I did a Psalm 42:9-11 straight at God. With my whole heart I said, "Why are you doing this to me? How long will you leave me suffering like this? What do you want me to do? Just tell me already!" I felt ridiculous at first. The thought of how my feeble voice must have sounded to the almighty God made my tears cease. I became still, not worried about the way I must have looked with tears streaming down my face. I was still—still enough to hear what came next.

In my heart I heard the question, "What do you want to do?

God turned my question around and asked me what I wanted. That question grounded me. I always thought about what he wanted from me, never about what I wanted for myself. I wish I could say in that moment I knew the answer, but I didn't know what I wanted. I didn't know who I was.

In my room that night, God answered my question with a question, and it was only the beginning of the work he was doing in me. Looking back, I realize I made a mistake in how I approached God. Surprisingly, getting mad at God was not the problem. The mistake was that I blended the lines between what I was supposed to do with my life and who I was. In other words, I mistook my calling for my identity. I thought if God just told me what he wanted me to do, I would have purpose. Quite the opposite was true. God led me to search my heart to see what I wanted to do with my life, only for me to go deeper to find out why. Yes, I wanted to help people know more about who Jesus was. That's what I wanted to do, but why did I want to do it? Yes, I wanted to be a stay-at-home mom. That's what I did, but why did I do it?

The "why" questions challenged me because they caused me to connect with my inner desires as well as my God-given design. Only through the deep seeking of those answers did I touch the surface of exploring who I really was. "Why" questions really do expose your heart, and your heart is linked to your identity when you ask God to come and make His dwelling place there. However, as Christians, we're often told not to ask "why" questions. We're told we should be comfortable with knowing that God has all the answers, and we should just be satisfied with that. Yet, even Jesus asked a "why" question. On the cross, with some of his final breaths, he asked the Father in a loud voice, "Why have you forsaken me?"[1] If Jesus asked a "why" question, I believe we can ask "why" questions also.

Fast forward five years later: my husband and I are planting a church in our hometown of Brooklyn. We are co-leading together, trusting God to be the head of our church. Reflecting on my life, I can confidently say I know how to describe myself. I'm a wife, a mother, a lead pastor, a preacher, and a church planter. Honestly though, the list goes on and on. I'm a class parent, a shower singer, and a decent cook. Not just one of those titles describes me— they all do. On this journey, I have learned a valuable lesson. While these titles describe me, they do not define me. They describe what I do but not who I am.

God showed me that people are more complex than society projects, and fitting people into a box is not God's plan for his children. I realized why I want to help people, not just that I do. I have a desire to witness people grow and reach their full God-given potential because transformation should be a regular part of life. I love to help people become their 2.0 Holy Spirit-led selves. I do that because God designed me to desire it. He created me that way. It's in my heart. It's how I'm wired to worship him.

---

1   Matthew 27:46, Mark 15:34.

As a woman, I often find people like to put me in a box that suits their expectations of who they want me to be in and outside of the church. To top things off, I do a really good job of doing that all on my own. People don't always mean to do this; they just do. It's humanity's way of having control. That night in my room though, I lost control, and thankfully I did. Only in that moment of desperation did God start me on the quest of discovery to find my true identity. In the simplest words: God explained to me that I am more. I'm more than I believe myself to be. I'm more than people say I am. I'm more than just one role I play in my life or the church. I don't fit in a box. I'm more.

I believe you are more too. You're more. You are immeasurably more than all you can ask for or imagine because of the power that is at work in you. God has a plan for you and a purpose, a calling and an identity. Remember the words of 1 Thessalonians 5:24 as you embark on your journey toward finding your identity: "The person that is calling you is faithful. He will do it."

Named + Known

SECTION 2

MISTAKEN IDENTITY

Expectations and an Identity Crisis

Heidy Tandy

"Heidy: we have no expectations of you here at this church."

Wait. What?

I had no idea how powerful those words would feel to me at the time, but this memory is etched in my brain. Sitting at a booth at the ever-so-delicious Real Hacienda in Anderson, Indiana, my husband's new boss, Paul, said that there were no expectations from him at our new church. I could not believe what he was saying.

Here's why this moment was so significant for me: I was twenty-six at the time and had been putting layers of expectations of others on me for my first five years of ministry. So of course, then, I had created this model pastor's wife in my head: these are the areas where she volunteers at the church; this is how often she opens up her home; this is what she is supposed to look like, sound like, be like.

To keep it real, I'm not sure if it was even about being a pastor's wife—I think it was even bigger than that for me. As a woman, where am I supposed to volunteer in church? What should my home be like? Am I supposed to look a certain way? Sound a certain way? Be a certain way? And on the other side, what can I say? What should I say? What if it's too much? I want to have it all together but not have it too together, because I want people to feel comfortable around me. It's like when someone says, "Act natural"—that in itself makes acting natural seem like the most difficult task in the world!

Maybe for you it's not that you have "pastor's wife expectations," but you have expectations about what you thought your life would look like. Maybe you thought you'd have kids, be married, or have gone to school. Maybe it has to do with the church that you have planted or will plant. Maybe you thought it would look a certain way or have taken a certain direction. Deep down in your spirit, you know that God is sovereign and doesn't make mistakes. Yet it can be so easy to fall into the trap of feeling as if I am mistaken, wrong, or invaluable.

In my story, I have allowed circumstances or the opinions of others to dictate what I think about myself. The reality is that if I am not carefully and intentionally creating space in my life to allow God to tell me who I am, I can easily fall into patterns of comparing myself to others, negative self talk, and an overall attitude of shame.

At the 2017 Bloom Retreat, I had one of those times where I fell back into patterns of mistaken identity. I was emceeing the retreat for the second year in a row and I was honored and excited to be part of one of my favorite events of the year. However, at the end of the first night I began to question my own leadership, comparing myself to the other speakers and leaders at the retreat. I questioned my ability to tell a good story, to lead, and to teach, and I wondered if I even had a place in the ministry that Bloom was doing. For the entire retreat, my headspace was an absolute mess.

I took some time after this retreat to process how I had been feeling with my trusted mentor, Vanessa Pugh. Sitting outside at my local coffee shop, I told her all of the unhealthy thoughts that I was having and the expectations and pressures that I was putting on myself to be like other women whom I admired. Vanessa isn't the type of mentor that lets me stay in the thought loops that can thwart my identity. She encouraged me to ask good questions of myself and of God. The question she always puts back on me (I love it and hate it at the same time) is: what is God trying to teach you in this situation?

I don't always want to be taught. Sometimes I don't want to learn lessons and I don't want to learn from my mistakes. Sometimes the work of getting out of negative or unhealthy thought patterns is more painful than the patterns themselves. I believe, however, it is worth it.

The prayer that I have prayed the most in the past few months is, "God will you remind me what you say about me? Tell me what you say about me." Time and time again I am pointed back to songs that answer this question. As someone who connects with the Lord most through music, I have clung to the words of the song, Who You Say I Am, by Hillsong Worship:

Who am I that the highest King
Would welcome me?
I was lost but He brought me in
Oh His love for me
Oh His love for me

Who the Son sets free
Oh is free indeed
I'm a child of God
Yes I am

Free at last, He has ransomed me
His grace runs deep
While I was a slave to sin
Jesus died for me
Yes He died for me

Who the Son sets free
Oh is free indeed
I'm a child of God

Yes I am
In my Father's house
There's a place for me
I'm a child of God
Yes I am

I am chosen
Not forsaken
I am who You say I am
You are for me
Not against me
I am who You say I am
I am who You say I am

Who the Son sets free
Oh is free indeed
I'm a child of God
Yes I am
In my Father's house
There's a place for me
I'm a child of God
Yes I am
I'm a child of God
Yes I am[1]

My kids have fallen in love with this song as well. Nothing brings me more joy than to hear my four and six-year-old belting out the bridge with fervor and intensity at the breakfast table. I pray that the words above, rooted in Scripture, would be written on their hearts as they grow into brave adults.

The process of being named and known, while not a linear process, includes getting it wrong sometimes or doing the work of reminding ourselves what God says about us. The women in this section have bravely shared their stories of mistaken identity: what happens when we allow others to define

---

1   Morgan, R., Fielding, B. (2018). Who You Say I Am [Recorded by Hillsong Worship]. Hillsong Music Australia and Capital Christian Music Group, CCLI Song #7102401.

us or attempt to be someone we aren't. My prayer for this section is that in the stories of others we would be spurred along to pursue the truth of our chosenness and freedom in Christ.

Don't Let the Title Fool You

Shannon Smith

I just needed to run a quick errand during lunch. No big deal. I exited out the glass double-doors of the high school to my outdated pickup truck. As I was unlocking the truck door, I heard yelling coming from the main entrance. I turned around to see the high school security officer running towards me. He was not happy. I turned my head to the left and the right hoping I was not the cause of his frustrated face. Unfortunately, I was the only one in the parking lot. I stood still as he raised his voice to tell me that I was not allowed to leave, to get back in the building, and go back to class. Wait. What? Go back to class? Sir, I'm a teacher.

It's been many years since that day. I still laugh about the embarrassing incident. Back then I was in my fourth year of teaching. I understand the mix-up. I was twenty-five years old teaching at a school where most of the students looked older than me. It was an innocent mistake. The security guard saw me from many yards away and assumed I was a student. It didn't matter that I was parked in a teacher's parking lot or that I had a name badge on. To the officer, I looked like a student, therefore, I was a student.

I left that job when Dan and I moved to start Momentum Church in Cleveland, Ohio. I am no longer a twenty-five year-old teacher mistaken for a student (stupid wrinkles), but I am still the victim of mistaken identity. The mistakes have happened in grocery stores, in coffee shops, and at our church services. They have happened while I've been in meetings, leading worship, or scrolling through social media. However, this time, I am not mistaken because of the way I look but because of the titles I hold as church planter, pastor's wife, and staff member.

I knew about the expectations that come with ministry titles before I ever married Dan. I'm a pastor's kid. When I was a teenager, my mom once told me, "Please don't marry a pastor." So guess what I went and did? I married a pastor! No worries, Mom. I assured her that my experience in church planting would be different than her experience in a traditional church.

That has been partly true. One of the beautiful things about church planting is that you get to set the tone and culture of the church from the very beginning. I don't feel the pressure to be a certain kind of church planter, pastor's wife, or staff member because I got to decide what my role looked like in the church and have stuck to it. My role is the same as everyone else's at Momentum— to move people forward to love God, love people, and make disciples who make disciples. I use my top three spiritual gifts of hospitality, leadership, and worship as a guide to where I should serve inside and outside of Momentum. It has been a freeing experience to not be stuck in a box where people expect you to dress a certain way, play the piano, and either lead or attend every event that takes place at the church.

Church planting, however, has not allowed me to escape all the problems that come along with those titles.

Experience this with me:

I walk down the hallway of the movie theater where church services are held. I've checked all three kids into MoKidz. I just finished nursing my youngest son and left my daughter screaming in her class. Oh boy. Now I have to rush to lead worship. There are people all around preparing to go into the service.

I get an email from a parent later in the day. "I'm upset with you. You're the pastor's wife and you ignored me in the hallway."

I'm in the local grocery store checking out. The grocery store has me a little nervous after having a creepy, scary stalker experience there. I am alert but a little on edge. I get an email later in the day from a man in the church. "I saw you at the grocery, and you didn't say hi. I didn't appreciate that."

I take six, count them, six kids to another church's sports camp. There are over one thousand children who attend this camp. Amidst a lot of chaos, I drop off my three kids and their friends. After doing a happy dance, I excitedly head to Starbucks for some quality time with friends. I'm scrolling on Facebook later that afternoon when I see a post by an old friend who has moved away. The lengthy post was about a pastor's wife from her previous church who did not stop to talk to her at a sports camp. She is very angry. Is she talking about me? Yep.

Now you may be thinking, Shannon, it sounds like you need to pay better attention to your surroundings. I know. I totally agree with you. I'm working on it. I tend to be very focused, shy, and a fast walker. The three together can be a bad combination. Once I walked right into a pole and broke my glasses.

But could it also be a case of mistaken identity? Over the years, I've come to realize that sometimes people see the title before they see me. Just like the security guard seeing me from afar and mistaking me for a student, some people see me from afar and mistake me for a church planter who never doubts, never fears, and always enjoys set-up and tear-down in a portable church. They mistake me for a pastor's wife who never gets angry, never curses, has resources for every topic, and has the time to meet the needs and wants of everyone in the church and the community. Most cases of mistaken identity are just innocent oversights that stem from good or bad past experiences, misconceptions, or expectations. I really do get it. However, over time, the mistakes can begin to cause problems.

Mistaken identity can actually be dangerous. You may have a security guard running after you in a parking lot or much worse. Can I be honest? One of the most devastating impacts that mistaken identity has had on me is a broken heart. When others fail to look past the titles, there is always a price to pay. Losing friends, people leaving the church, and members being upset with me because I have not met their expectations have left a trail of emotional trauma and anxiety in my life. It's no wonder why so many in ministry seek counseling.

However, this does not exclude me from carrying out the mission God has set before me so I push on, knowing that my true identity is never a mystery to Jesus. Isn't that amazing? My true identity is never a mystery to Jesus. Others may mistake my identity. I may go through spells where I feel like I have no identity. But to Jesus, it is never a mystery. I am a child of God. For those that do mistake my title for my identity, I am confident that if they get close enough to me to see my badge, they will be able to read the words: child of God, mother, wife, sister, coworker, and friend and eventually be able to separate me from the ministry titles. We'll have a good laugh over it.

Now to work on getting rid of these wrinkles.

Loaves and Fishes

Jessica Moerman

How can you be a scientist and serve God?

This was the question I asked myself over and over again the summer before my first year of college. Growing up in the foothills of the Great Smoky Mountains in Tennessee, it's hard not to be in awe of God's creation, and after years wandering along rhododendron-lined mountain streams and under towering rocky cliffs, a deep curiosity for how all this was made took hold of me. But I couldn't see how majoring in geology fit with my earlier calling to serve God in ministry. At the time, I thought the only way to serve God with your whole life was to become a missionary or a preacher, and I couldn't see how a rock-hammer-toting geologist played any part advancing the kingdom of God. Yet I kept feeling this pull to study God's creation through science. As the start of college loomed larger, I was in a vise over what seemed like a choice between either obedience to God in the calling he had placed on my life or turning my back on it to pursue this deep passion for science that had welled up in me.

I then had a conversation that set the trajectory of my life: I shared my conflicting feelings with a church youth leader (can I get a shoutout for youth leaders?!), who, unbeknownst to me, turned out to be a geologist. I was stunned to meet someone pursuing both science and ministry. He told me something that put my heart at total ease: that God places within us unique passions to serve him with in ways and places unique to each of us. He also told me that as we surrender ourselves in obedience to God, we can trust that he "is working in [us], giving [us] the desire and the power to do what pleases him."[1] These words were so freeing. I realized God was the source of my deep curiosity and drive to understand his created world and that I was mistaken in assuming my calling to serve his kingdom was incompatible with my passion for science. In that moment, I began to trust that he had a plan and purpose for giving me these twin callings and desires; it wasn't a choice of "either/or" but rather "both/and," if I had the courage to step into this unknown territory.

Looking back, deciding my college major felt so consequential because I too often define myself by what I do—scientist, pastor's wife, church planter, mom. I also tend to tie my sense of self-worth to how well I feel I'm doing in those roles. Together, this makes for quite the roller coaster ride when I forget to anchor myself in God's truth: hanging on the highs of success and sinking into the deep lows of self-doubt when failures inevitably occur.

Never have I experienced more ups and downs than during our season of church planting. In 2015, over a five-month timespan, I defended my PhD dissertation, gave birth to our beautiful son, moved over 600 miles away from friends and family in Atlanta to Washington, DC to start our church, Grace Capital City, and began a new research position at Johns Hopkins University, commuting over an hour each way to and from Baltimore.

This was exhilarating, and it was exhausting. Yes, it was all I could have dreamed of: the opportunity to conduct cutting edge research at a top university, partnering with my husband to launch a new church in a city that desperately needs them, and most of all, being a mother to our gorgeous son. But increasingly these roles began to feel at odds with each other. How could I be a successful mother when work and church were taking so much

---

1   Philippians 2:13, NLT.

time away from my son? How could I be a successful church planter and pastor's wife when work plus a commute kept me from meeting up with new church members for coffee and when chasing after an increasingly mobile toddler kept me from even finishing a single conversation? How could I be a successful scientist when I couldn't spend 24/7 in the lab running analyses and writing reports like my colleagues? Each role seemed to steal success from the others, causing me to deeply question my worth in it all.

Stressed and striving, this wasn't God's promise. As I floundered, God reminded me of a conversation I had with a professor in grad school who was also a leader at our church in Atlanta. Impressed by his ability to balance family and church leadership with a thriving and successful research program, I wanted to know how he did it. His path, he said, was to seek God first, set clear boundaries, and trust the Lord to provide. He sought God first to ensure he stayed in alignment with all God called him to, and he set clear boundaries so that work and research didn't encroach on time with family and church. This of course meant he spent less time in the lab than his colleagues, but he trusted God to take those hours and provide all that was needed. Just as Jesus used a boy's small offering of loaves and fishes to feed thousands, he trusted God could do more with those fewer hours he clocked in than what he himself could accomplish striving in his own strength.

The reminder of my friend's words gave great comfort but also challenged me deeply. It forced me to come to grips with my own fears and insecurities about failing to live up to my own lofty expectations as well as come to terms with the limits of my own capacity. I have finite energy and limited hours in the day with so many responsibilities competing for every one of those hours. In so many ways I was just like the boy with the loaves and fish. I had so little to offer, yet there were so many 'mouths' to feed. The follow-up questions were equally challenging: What would it mean if I couldn't meet the picture of success in everything I sought to do? What would the people in our new church think of me? What would my family think of me? What would God think of me? Would I be enough?

Of course, the beauty of the story of Jesus feeding the five thousand is exactly that the little boy's offering is not enough. It's not even close to enough. There's no way five loaves and two fish could feed a crowd that size. And yet he was willing to bring them. And from that act of offering, God filled the space and provided for the need.

Much of my own journey of identity has been learning to be ok with my limitations and learning that God is so pleased with the loaves and fishes I can offer; stretching myself too thin, striving to be the best at all things takes my focus from what God has uniquely purposed for me. I have also learned that any gaps left by my limited capacity are actually opportunities for church members to step up into leadership and exercise their gifts and talents, opportunities they perhaps may not have if I am filling the space. There are certainly some roles that only I can fill, but part of the beauty of the body of Christ is that there are other roles that someone else can fill.

A verse that's encouraged me when I've felt discouraged has been Psalm 73:26: "Though my flesh and my heart may fail, the Lord is the strength of my life, and my portion forever." Another way of saying 'God is our portion' is that 'God is enough.' When I've been overwhelmed by my limitations and feelings of failure, when I feel like I am not enough, it has been a great comfort to remember that God is enough. He is enough to fill the spaces, he is enough to lead his church, he is enough for my family, he is enough for the people in our city, he has been enough on my journey so far, and I choose to trust that he will be enough as he leads us on.

Duck Duck Grey Duck

Stacie Salva

I am a small town, midwestern girl who grew up attending the same country church in Southeast Minnesota that my father attended growing up. I have memories of my grandmother playing the organ in church and passing me Chiclets. There was no such thing as Children's Ministry back then, at least where I lived. I grew up sitting in the wooden pews or following in my grandmother's footsteps and playing the piano.

As I became an adult, I started to realize that people in Minnesota do things a little differently than people in other parts of the country. Remember that favorite childhood game Duck-Duck-Goose where all the kids sit in a circle on the floor, and one person walks around saying, "Duck, duck, duck, duck... goose"? Well, if you grew up in Minnesota, that game was called Duck-Duck-Grey Duck. It went something like this: "Red duck, blue duck, yellow duck... grey duck!" Being selected "grey duck" meant that you were the odd man out. Who knew that children in Minnesota are the only children in the country that play the game this way? Now I think I grew up playing it in the best and most creative way. That being said, I have spent a lot of my life feeling like a grey duck.

Our church planting journey began back in 1999. My husband, Toney, and I met at a small Christian college in Southwest Missouri and remained in that area after graduation. In 1999 we were both working at a large church where we were very comfortable. Toney was the Children and Family Pastor, and I was the Preschool Director. We had built our first house and had our first child, Tanner. We had grandparents that moved to the area to help babysit. Life was good.

Then, the call came. We were invited to help start a new urban church in Lowell, Massachusetts. Why would we do that? We had it made where we were. We could picture ourselves staying with this church for many years to come. However, God had other plans. We traded in that house for an apartment, a wonderful church family for a church that didn't exist, and job security for raising support to live on. We weren't in the suburbs anymore. There was often vomit in the lobby of our apartment building; drug deals happened outside our windows, and our neighbor (with whom we shared a laundry room) had a six-inch-thick police file. When he broke into our church office down the street we were told by local law enforcement, "I would keep women and children away from this guy." Well, he lived across the hall! This small town Minnesota girl had a lot to learn!

The three years we served planting that church were some of my toughest years personally but also some of the best I had ever experienced. I was out of my comfort zone in every facet of life. During our time in New England, our daughter Haley was born, and something inside me was born too. I began to take initiative to do what I could do for the church from home with two small kids and rather accidentally, started a women's ministry. While I served and was a leader, I never considered myself a leader. I never quite felt like I fit in with other women or had the qualities that a leader should have. In my mind, I was never good enough. I always felt like a grey duck.

Through that experience, my husband was given the opportunity to be a lead planter and was asked to start a church just north of Pittsburgh, Pennsylvania. God provided a house for us and we moved once again into an area we had never been. Early on, the management team suggested that I consider being the church's Children and Family Pastor. In my mind this was going to be a temporary role to help get things started. Well, I'm still doing it fifteen years later!

I love being the Children Family Pastor now, but I didn't always feel that way. I still struggled to consider myself a leader. I could fill this chapter with all the ways I am not good enough to lead. I always compared myself with others who were more dominant leaders in ministry, and I always felt like I came up short. I spent many years discontent, wondering if I should be doing something outside of the church instead. I didn't embrace who God made me to be and how he was using me. I didn't see the value and influence I had or the privilege it was to invite and equip others to serve in those early years. After all, I was just a grey duck.

Over the years, that feeling of not being good enough to lead has slowly diminished. I went through a period of time where I deliberately withdrew from the busyness of life and focused on what was most important. I cut out the non-essentials from my schedule. I visited with a counselor for about a year, spent more time in prayer, read, and simply slowed down to do the work of recognizing and dealing with wounds that had been ignored for far too long. One of the many books that was most helpful to me was When the Heart Waits by Sue Monk Kidd. When referring to the activity of waiting she says:

> *"It's a vibrant, contemplative work. It means descending into self, into God, into the deeper labyrinths of prayer. It involves listening to disinherited voices within, facing the wounded holes in the soul, the denied and undiscovered, the places one lives falsely. It means struggling with the vision of who we really are in God and molding the courage to live that vision."*[1]

The work of waiting is where transformation begins.

That period of time helped me become more of my true self. It helped me to become more honest with myself. I have learned (and continue to learn) that my identity and my confidence come from God. It isn't about pleasing others or trying to be like someone else. I need to be who God created me to be. I can be confident that God has given me this amazing opportunity to lead and that he is using me. That brings true fulfillment.

---

1   Kidd, Sue Monk. When the Heart Waits: Spiritual Direction for Life's Sacred Questions. Harper-SanFrancisco, 2006.

God had given me the opportunity for leadership and influence. Leadership and influence really is all about helping people, right? You don't need a specific skill set or degree to do that. We just need to be willing to serve and step into the influence God has given us. We need to trust that he will give us what we need to lead. He will equip us. Trust that he has put us in the right place, at the right time to do what he has made us to do. I have had the privilege of baptizing many of my children's volunteers over the years and then see many of them baptize kids in their classes! I have seen both of my own children baptize others. There is nothing more fulfilling than that!

Through nearly twenty years of church planting, we have had our share of struggles, disappointments, and victories. We have experienced people leaving the church, closing campuses, pay cuts, cancer, family deaths, marriage struggles and counseling, and being months away from breaking ground on a building only to have the entire project suddenly come to an end. Even through all of the struggles, we have seen more than six hundred people give their lives to Christ in baptism.

The church we started has planted five additional daughter churches in our region, assisted with four internationally, and started two mission organizations in El Salvador. All because we said yes to stepping out of our comfort zones to plant a church.

Our son is now living in southwest Missouri himself and attending the same Christian college my husband and I attended so many years ago. And guess what his major is? Church planting! I guess what he experienced growing up meant something to him. My husband has recently transitioned from being the Lead Pastor of the church we started fifteen years ago to working full-time with Stadia Church Planting as the Northeast Regional Director helping to start even more churches! I remain at the church in my role as Children and Family Pastor because my time serving and leading is not over yet!

Looking back over our journey I am amazed at how God has worked and how he has provided every step of the way. His plan wasn't always easy or what I thought it should be, but his plan has always been so much bigger and better than my own. When we made that first big move back in 1999, we were reminded of the story of Joshua. God wanted him to lead the Israelites across the Jordan river at flood stage in Joshua 3. Why would anyone do that? It didn't make sense. God rarely makes sense to our limited perspective. We don't always see the bigger story that God is writing. Joshua 3:5 says, "Consecrate yourselves, for tomorrow the Lord will do amazing things among you." God is all about doing things that are too hard for us to do on our own. If God can use this grey duck from Minnesota with all of her insecurities and doubts about who God made her to be, he can use you too. Because Christ is in you, you are enough.

SECTION 3

UNEXPECTED IDENTITY

Identity Versus Biography

Heidy Tandy

"If you're not careful, you can confuse your identity with your biography." – John O'Donohue[1]

"That. Is. So. Good!" I yelled to myself, alone in the car. If you're like me, when I'm driving alone and hear such juicy nuggets of wisdom, I frequently and loudly affirm to myself, "That. Is. So. Good." The car yelling was caused by the quote referenced above. CJ Cassiota quoted O'Donohue on a podcast I was listening to recently, and I haven't been able to get it out of my head.

Unfortunately, the quote sent me into a tailspin about this whole section; I wasn't sure I could even write the story I had in mind for this opening. I thought that even titling this section "unexpected identity" could potentially fall into the trap of confusing our identity with our biography. Often I do allow the current circumstances in my life to dictate my attitude, daily rhythms, and, if I'm not careful, my identity.

---

1 Downs, Annie F., host. "100. CJ Casciotta." That Sounds Fun with Annie F. Downs., Relevant Podcast Network, 17 Sept. 2018. https://relevantmagazine.com/podcast/episode-100-cj-casciotta/.

So I went back to the initial definition of identity I have used for this entire book project: identity is the distinguishing characteristics or personality of an individual, one's sense of self. Furthermore, these characteristics are ultimately God-breathed into us—he knows all of our qualities, how our brains work, even our Enneagram numbers. Nothing is unexpected to him. However, in the first five years of church planting, there sure have been some unexpected parts in my story.

Prior to church planting, I knew it would be hard. I knew that building something from the ground up, moving to a town where we knew no one, and building trust in a community that had a rather painful history with the church would be difficult. That part I knew. What I wasn't prepared for was the unexpected shift that our family would navigate after our church plant had already begun.

On September 8, 2016, at the age of four our son was diagnosed with Autism. This day was the culmination of two and a half years of asking myself:

Shouldn't he be talking already?

Are these meltdowns the terrible twos, or is it more than that?

Why doesn't he seem to be progressing like the other kids?

Are the therapies and interventions working?

I also asked God a lot of questions during this time too:

Do I have what it takes to give our boy what he needs?

How will I make it through this day?

What does this mean for his adult life?

Instead of the car yelling, as mentioned above, I found myself doing a lot more car crying. Sometimes at the end of the day during this season, I would go for a drive just to get out of the house while my husband stayed home with the kids. I love where we live—in five minutes I can view the beautiful skyline of Cincinnati, or if I travel in a different direction, I can be on country roads in the beautiful hills of Kentucky. So in the evenings I would just drive, literally crying out to God because the journey I was on just felt so incredibly unexpected. Looking back, these were sacred drives. I didn't necessarily feel as if anything was solved during these trips, but I was able to check in with the Lord, experience a change of scenery, and breathe.

Post-diagnosis I rarely took time to sit and breathe during the day. I wanted to learn about appropriate therapies and how to empower those around me to understand our son, and I spent dozens of hours on the phone trying to navigate the medical system now that we had an official diagnosis. The learning curve was extraordinarily steep. And my grip of control was exceedingly tight.

Let me introduce you to Mary. Mary is my counselor. I started seeing Mary on my husband's birthday in 2016. (I thought it was a great idea to get myself therapy for his birthday—everybody wins!) Through one of the biggest challenges of my life, I was able to have regular appointments where I was able to receive faith-based feedback and care from a licensed professional. While it didn't change the circumstances, I gained valuable insights that shifted my perspective completely, particularly around how I have a small (large) tendency to overly control.

Though it is painful to say, if it wasn't Autism, it would be something else in my life that would wreck me. There would be something else that would prove me wrong in thinking that if I just do the right things, say the right things, parent the right way (even do church the right way!), then I would be perfect, worthy, okay. Jesus tells us, "In this world you will have trouble, but take heart, I have overcome the world."[2] I know I'm not the exception to that rule, but I sure try to avoid trouble with control. Clearly, that does not work. But I sure try!

I'm not going to wrap up this chapter introduction with a beautiful bow. The reality is that I don't have one, although I much prefer stories with a happy ending (don't even get me started on the movie The Breakup with Vince

---

2   John 16:33.

Vaughn and Jennifer Aniston). While the learning curve isn't as steep and we are learning more of our rhythm as a family, we have had to make changes in how we do life at home and even what my role looks like at church. These decisions have been difficult at times to make, but, like we say in our family, we can do hard things.

My identity isn't primarily found in being the parent of a kiddo with special needs. My sense of self and my characteristics were present in me long before this story began. I consider certain elements of this unexpected part of my story a gift. I see God's kindness all over the ways he has shown up in the last few years: a last-minute meal, the generosity of others, and specific people in our lives that uniquely understand developmental disabilities. Our relational God and his grace have been sufficient for me.

The stories in this section are from women in church planting who have wrestled with this notion that life does not always look the way we thought it would. I pray that in the honest stories in this section, you would begin to see the ways where God has used your biography to remind you of your identity.

Freedom From the Lies

Sheila Brown

Remember back when we were in high school and we couldn't wait to get our driver's license, go on our first date, attend prom, and then graduate? Maybe for some of us it was going off to college next or finding a job, then getting married, and finally starting a family. It felt like time went by so slow back then.

Looking back, I can honestly say who I was, thankfully, has changed over the years. I remember in high school always wanting to fit in and my mom telling me that one day after I graduate I would more than likely never see most of these kids again that I was trying to impress with the things I had and did. Boy, was she right!

We all have an identity! On my journey to discover my true identity, I have learned that where we look to find our identity is most important. I am forty-three years old. My husband, Jeremy, and I have been married now for almost twenty-three years, and we have three teenage daughters. Since getting married we have lived in three different states. Our last move took us to Tennessee where we planted our church that is now eight years old. I always knew I wanted to get married and have kids, so the transition of becoming a wife and mom was really not a huge deal for me. Don't get me wrong—marriage and parenting are work, but my identity in being a wife and mom was something I had dreamed of for years.

For some people, turning thirty is hard, but for me I had a baby and two toddlers, so that milestone didn't seem to be much of a struggle for me. But, when I turned forty just a few years ago, that was really hard! I was so overwhelmed with the thought that in just ten short years I would be fifty, could easily have a daughter or two married, and could possibly even have grandkids! All of a sudden time seemed to be going by so quickly! Our oldest daughter also got her license that same year, which left me feeling like I was not needed as much as I was before. I didn't recognize it at the time, but what I was really struggling with was trying to figure out who I was.

Our identity is what allows us to be unique from everyone else, and there are a lot of factors that go into making up our identities. Sometimes we even allow our circumstances to tell us who we are—even those circumstances that we have no control over at all. I would never have guessed that in my forties I would be struggling with my identity. I honestly felt like I was losing who I was because for years my identity had been wrapped up in my kids and being a pastor's wife.

That same year I turned forty, our church was in the throes of a building project. We were very excited to no longer have to set-up and tear-down every week after having done that for the last five years. The funny thing about church planting is that you learn to wear a lot of different hats. Over the years, I have had numerous roles at our church as a volunteer. I suppose you fill in where you are needed until you can find someone that is able to take over that role for you. The problem with this is that you can end up agreeing to roles that you're not gifted for or (worse!) you don't enjoy doing, which can cause you to burn out very quickly. So I found myself not only struggling with my identity at home, but also struggling with what my purpose and role was at our church too!

One day my husband and I were talking, and he very gently and kindly encouraged me to go and talk to a doctor. It took me some time before I got enough courage to find a doctor and make an appointment to go in to talk about the possibility that I could be depressed. Of course, looking back now I can see that I had been struggling with depression over the last couple of years. There were times when life was stressful, and I could manage just fine. Then there were times when I was so overwhelmed that I felt like the life I knew was like a big snowball getting bigger and bigger as it rolled down a hill completely out of control.

I wasn't sleeping much and was so unmotivated. I eventually began to take medication for depression, which for a time seemed to be doing the trick. The truth is, there was more going on than just a chemical imbalance. What I didn't recognize was the enemy was speaking some pretty big lies to me that I believed as truth, which left me feeling very sad, lonely, overwhelmed, resentful, and guilty for having all of those feelings.

I was so tired of walking into church, putting on my happy face, and sitting by myself that I honestly just didn't even want to go anymore. I can remember numerous times sitting in church on the verge of tears and feeling so miserable and honestly so resentful towards the people at our church! Did they even care that we moved away from our families to serve here, or did they just take it for granted that we would be there the next time they needed someone to talk to? One night Jeremy and I were talking, and I told him I did not know how much longer I could continue doing ministry; I was feeling completely burned out. That particular conversation we had that night led to many other conversations in the days and weeks to come with friends, family, and a counselor.

Our mind really is a battlefield! I am learning daily that I have to take every single thought captive. When I don't take every thought captive, I begin to make agreements with the enemy, which is what was happening. I lived my life in fear, saying no to things that God was calling me to because of the lies I believed about myself that left me feeling so insecure. The enemy knows our weakness, and I believe there is a little truth in the lies he tells us so that it makes it easier for us to believe them. For years—and I do mean years—I was making agreements with the enemy. I was allowing those strongholds to hold me back and take me prisoner locked in chains of deception. When we believe the lies, we begin to view ourselves and our circumstances through those lies. It literally paralyzes us. If we don't take our thoughts captive, they will take us captive. It leaves us feeling stuck with no hope. Here I was telling others there is hope for their situations but feeling like I had no hope for my own.

A while back I was at a retreat and the speaker talked about the lies the enemy tells us and the strongholds that form when we believe them. In Revelation 2:17 it says, "I will give to each one a white stone, and on the stone will be engraved a new name that no one understands except the one who receives it." The questions I needed to ask were: who does God say I am, and what false identities do I need to let go of? When I finally asked God who he said I was, I really felt like he told me the name he gave me was Worthy.

Later that day when I searched for the meaning of worthy, I found that it means having enough good qualities to be considered important and useful. For years I had struggled with the questions: am I really enough, am I important, and am I valued? Those questions went all the way back to my days in high school and even earlier. How good of God to remind me of who I am! I now have a little white stone with the name Worthy written on it sitting next to my sink in my bathroom so I can see it everyday and be reminded of my identity in Christ.

When we look to the people in our church, to our staff, to our spouse, or to our children for our identity, we will never be enough. But when we seek him for our identity, we can have confidence in who he says we are.

This summer my husband and I were able to take our first ever month-long sabbatical. For an entire month we had no responsibilities—no social media, no returning emails or phone calls, no appointments, nothing! It was wonderful! Don't get me wrong; I love what we do, and I am thankful I get to spend my forever with Jeremy on mission to win people for Jesus, but church planting is hard. It's good, but at times it is really hard.

I just want to encourage you that if any of this resonates with you, let me be the first person to say it is okay to seek a medical professional for help. There are times, especially as we age and live in this broken world, that we need medicine as treatment. It is okay to treat your anxiety and depression with medicine just like you would if you had high blood pressure or diabetes. Also let me encourage you to find a good counselor that can help you unpack all that you are experiencing and dealing with. If you are married, have conversations and be honest with your spouse.

The older I get the more I recognize that time really does go so quickly. I just want to enjoy every moment in every season I am in. The only way I can do that is when I recognize who I am in him. There is so much freedom and confidence that comes when we find our true identity and stop believing the lies from the enemy.

Named + Known

What's Stopping You?

Rachel Short

"What is stopping you from just accepting that you are an influential woman leader called by God?"

That was the question from one of my CPAC (Church Planting Assessment Center) assessors that hit me like a ton of bricks. He had struck a chord.

Through tears, I tried to work up the courage to say what my heart was feeling—that my relationship status had made me unqualified for church planting.

As a relatively confident single woman with many married friends, my relationship status had never bothered me in this way before. But this church planting environment was unchartered territory. The week of assessment, I looked around, and all I saw were married women; it seemed as if everyone but me had a partner in ministry for the arduous terrain ahead, whereas I felt as if I was on my own.

What had I gotten myself into?

Several months prior to CPAC, Marc Lucenius, one of the pastors of my church, announced that he and his wife Kathleen were launching Project 938 in West Chester, Pennsylvania. I had met Marc a few times at church, and since I lived in downtown West Chester, he and Kathleen invited me to coffee. Flattered by their request, I suggested one of my favorite breakfast spots, Market Street Grill. They shared about their vision for planting in the very unchurched area of West Chester. Studies aside, I knew that "unchurched" must have been true about the area because it had taken me forever to find a church when I had moved from Texas two and a half years prior. As they were talking about the community of West Chester and planting churches on the East Coast, it was like God began tugging on my heart, whispering, "Listen."

Our breakfast was interesting timing because I had just been praying (and asking others to pray as well) for a new career path. Friends and family started to encourage me towards the direction of ministry. Ministry had always been my heart's desire, but the question of when was still up in the air. Marc asked me to join them at Exponential a few weeks later, and before I knew it, we were talking about a full-time position. And, in September of 2017, I left my corporate career, went through CPAC, and started full-time October 1.

We hit the ground running with pre-launch season. The marketing, outreach, events, conversations, meetings, meetings, and more meetings were all underway. And on February 4, 2018, we launched Project 938 on Super Bowl Sunday in West Chester. Yes, the Eagles can thank us for winning the Super Bowl! It was an incredible memory that I will never forget.

Post-grand opening, we were in the thick of it—launching small groups, planning Easter, building out serving teams, praying for leaders, and just figuring out how we work and how we work together.

"Outreach and Connections Director" has meant a lot of things depending on the day (#churchplanting). But, my primary role has been developing the system for connecting people into the life of our church. In one short year, I've done everything from building a communications team to launching a connections strategy to preaching a sermon. Every day is a new day, and I have loved (almost) every moment of it.

But in September of 2018, a year later, I found myself feeling alone and out of place. Loneliness was not new to me. I had knocked down its door many times, but this loneliness was of a different breed. This loneliness took me off guard, and often times it was combined with fear. I never thought of myself as a particularly anxious person, but suddenly, I knew what struggling with anxiety felt like.

What had happened? How could the most rewarding, life-giving journey of church planting simultaneously cause me to question every aspect of my identity in Christ? Hadn't I already dealt with my junk? I was supposed to be leading newcomers and the unchurched community to the foot of the cross to find a new identity, yet I had forgotten mine. All the things I had thought I'd worked through—perfectionism, achievement, control—seemed mentally pervasive. Despite my feelings, I knew the truth: God had called me to this journey, and he would not abandon me.

Without a shadow of a doubt, I knew God had ordained the decision, church planting, and vocational ministry. Our team had been my greatest joy over the past year. But, I had no idea my new career path would be this hard. Of course starting a new church in an unchurched area would be challenging, but I was naive to the road ahead. The road ahead was filled with new experiences, opportunities, relationships, and hopes and dreams. But it was also filled with new insecurities, fears, uncertainties, and pain points. The insecurities always began with fleeting thoughts:

I'm not old enough for them (the launch team) to respect me.

What if the men resent me for teaching on a Sunday?

I am not assertive enough to lead our teams forward.

If I were married, I would have more credibility.

If I were a man, maybe my voice would be heard.

I realize these thoughts are not based in truth and not reflective of 99.9% of our church. But, these were the thoughts that kept me up at night when I lost my breath while giving announcements or forgot the vision part of the vision-casting talk I had a prepared. These thoughts would turn into long podcasts hosted by the enemy, telling me I needed to work harder on my public speaking before I could earn the right to take the stage, I needed to be more like so-and-so in order to be seen as a leader, or I needed to hurry up and get married so I could be perceived as more of an authority.

I found myself losing control of my mental faculties and sitting in a counselor's office with a long list of why I thought I was there. God had used starting a church to force me to grapple with my own brokenness in a way I had never experienced before. In my approval-driven, performance leadership that sought to reach the masses with the gospel of Jesus, I had forgotten the gospel for myself.

The song "Wake Me Up When September Ends" by Green Day would play on repeat in my head. One evening that September, I went for a walk—Jesus has always used nature as a special sanctuary for me. While walking, I tried to think of someone who wasn't in my church planting world (or in Texas, my home state) to call nearby. After what felt like an eternity of pondering my mental rolodex of non-church planting folks, I thought of Elizabeth. I called her and asked if I could come over so she could pray with me. I was looking for someone to help me feel less isolated and alone.

As I cried in her arms, Elizabeth begged God on my behalf. I do not believe Satan is around every corner, but I am a firm believer in spiritual warfare. This battle between flesh and blood had felt like it was taking me out. Elizabeth prayed all of the things my heart was feeling and my mind was acknowledging but only the Holy Spirit could voice. She prayed for God to meet me in my singleness. She prayed for God to strengthen me in my loneliness. And she prayed that I could find rest in the certainty of Jesus as my ministry partner. At the end of her prayer, she said, "We bring these things to you and lay them at the foot of the cross, dear King." In every way, I felt poured out at the foot of the cross.

As Christians, at the foot of the cross is a great place to be—vulnerable and completely dependent on God. But my vulnerability had felt crippling. Never before had I felt so exposed. Four years in the corporate world had showed me a different kind of vulnerability. Sure, meeting business goals, climbing the corporate ladder, and trying not to look like the dumbest person in the room definitely felt vulnerable and kept me on my toes.

However, I was able to keep my personal life pretty separate from my professional life, and despite priding myself on being a fairly open person, I liked having different categories for life. In church planting, my categories had dissipated, and after a year of church planting under my belt, I felt like Eve in the Garden looking for the largest tree I could find to hide behind. No longer did I want to be seen—something I so desired in previous jobs. No longer did I want to be known—also one of my former prayer requests while working in the corporate world. I just wanted to go back to a sense of normalcy, even though I knew normal was an illusion.

In this unexpected season, I clung to the words of Isaiah 41:10: "Fear not, for I am with you; do not be dismayed, for I am your God. I will strengthen you; I will help you, I will uphold you with my righteous right hand."

One morning as birds chirped outside my office window and my eyes gazed upon the paper calendar on my bulletin board, I saw the good news: tomorrow was October 1. A sigh of relief combined with the Holy Spirit's peace began resting on my soul. Phew. I had made it through September, only by the grace of God.

A year after I switched careers, I still talk to Jesus about that question my CPAC assessor asked. What is stopping me from just accepting that I am an influential woman leader called by God?

My assessors spoke truth to me in that moment and really loved me in a way that I will never forget. Honestly, I still feel some days (and through tears) that my relationship status does make me unqualified. I long for a godly husband to partner with in ministry. I desire a family of my own. I pray for the day when I can say, "I'm with him."

The story I began believing that tough September was that a husband would make it all better. A husband would take away all of my other leadership insecurities and give me the confidence I needed for church planting. Oh, the lies we believe in the midst of our pain and insecurity. The story I began believing was nothing like God's story. The story God is writing has friends coming to faith, broken lives being restored, and the Holy Spirit teaching me to trust him. The story God is writing has powerful moments of Jesus rescuing me and calling me to be that influential woman leader called by God. The story God is writing has given me an unexpected identity found in Jesus. And so when others ask, regardless of my relationship status, I can honestly say, "I'm with him."

The Importance of Turtleneck Sweaters

Michaell Dupin

A single mom at the age of 18.

Talk about unexpected. Now I did realize how this happens in life, but giving my life to Jesus at a young age and being heavily connected to a loving church community that was like family, I never imagined this would be where I would find myself. As reality began to sink in, I will never forget sitting on the bathroom floor and sobbing as I tried to figure out how in the world I would care for another human life. I will never forget walking into the garage to find my dad just standing there with tears streaming down his face because this was not the future he had envisioned for his daughter. Still so clear in my mind are the whispers around me as people who cared about me tried to figure out how this could have happened and began to speculate what my future would now look like.

For the next nine months, my emotions seemed to hit me in waves: waves sometimes washing over me lightly as I tried to figure my way forward and other times slamming into me with such a force that I felt like the air was knocked out of me. I felt fear of what the future would look like and inadequate for the responsibility ahead. I felt ashamed because I knew this was not what God had intended for me or the life forming inside of me. And many times I felt despair wondering how I could ever forgive myself for walking outside of what God had designed for my life.

In addition to my own feelings, I also had to face the decisions made by the church I loved, concerning me. I was removed from my student leadership roles, as well as singing up front. I was scheduled to go before the board of elders and also asked to share my sin with the entire church. Now I fully understand that there needed to be consequences to my actions, that I had not lived up to my responsibility as a leader to my peers, but I could not figure out how just my sin required a public confession in front of everyone. All of this that was being required of me only added to the struggle I was facing of finding a way to forgive myself and see hope in the future.

As I look back at this time, I realize there are often moments in our lives where we (or others) attempt to count ourselves out—where mistakes have been made or circumstances occur that cause us to doubt the impact we can have or the plans God has for us. But what I have found over and over is that God never sees it that way. Nothing catches him off guard, even the most unexpected moments to us. There is still this beautiful story he has for our lives that just might have a different plot than we originally imagined. He has a future handcrafted for us and an impact for us to make that often times surprises us. We might take detours; we might listen to the lies of the enemy coming through the voice of others or our own minds, but God has this patient and persistent way of bringing people and circumstances into our lives that help point us back to what we were created for.

Laurie was that person for me. Laurie had walked through the same circumstances I was currently in, and she was now a woman of great influence in our church. She gave up a lot of time and energy in this season to walk beside me. She fought on my behalf to lessen the actions being taken by the church; she stood with my family and I as I sat in a room surrounded by the leadership of the church to share the mistakes I had made. But most importantly, she showed up in my darkest moments to remind me that God still loved me just the same, that he had a great future for my daughter and

I, and that He would still use me in ways I couldn't possibly see at the time. I believe it was this relationship that planted the thought somewhere deep within me that I could still be a woman of influence for him. However, had you told me at the time that my leadership in the church would be restored and in even greater measure, and that one day I would be a church planter, I would have thought you were confused and quite possibly out of your mind.

Over the next few years there were people who invested in me and were willing to give me leadership as I desired to help students at the age where my struggles really began. It might have been fairly unconventional, but they allowed me to serve with my beautiful three-year-old daughter, Savannah, right beside me. It was also these same people investing in me who thought they would help my future along and pair me up with a youth pastor at camp who ended up becoming my husband and the father to Savannah that I had been praying for.

As we began our ministry together with a move across the country and a position at my father-in-law's church, I was given more and more leadership. I wish I could say I stepped into these new opportunities with ease, but my doubts of whether or not I should be in this role and whether I had the ability to lead the people looking at me for direction often crowded my mind. When I was asked to lead the small group ministry, I was honored to be asked. I had done this for students, and I loved giving a place for people to find community, so maybe a natural step was to do the same for adults.

The anxiousness quickly set in, however, when I was told I would start by meeting the small group "coaches" every Wednesday morning at 6 am. 6am? Yes, 6 am because all of the "coaches" had been given this title because they were the elders of a fairly large church and also very successful businessmen that needed to move on with their day. So, not only was this my first time really leading adults, it would be a table full of men—men who were extraordinary leaders in their own right. If you could look back at my shopping receipts at the time, you would find that I had to heavily invest in turtleneck sweaters (I think they were "in" at the time) because the minute I sat in front of these men to "train and develop" them as small group coaches, I would feel this warmth move from my neck to my face, and if I was not fully covered, you would see big red blotches form all over my chest and neck.

Nonetheless, it was through a wardrobe change and the belief of others, especially my husband, that I began to slowly grow more comfortable speaking in front of others. It was God gently reminding me that my identity was to be firmly rooted in him, which meant my success in this role was not the most important thing. Up to that point, I had thought my best contribution was behind the scenes. But as I began to develop others and speak in smaller settings more often, I began to realize (in spite of the nerves, the sick stomach, and the blotchiness) I really loved it. I will always remember a few specific men in leadership roles who went out of their way to encourage me, to speak belief in me, and to help me see ways I could continue to grow in the leadership I had been given. I realize this is not everyone's experience as they begin to grow as a female leader in the church, which is why I am even more thankful for these people who may not even know their impact on my life.

As we started to seek God for what was next in our lives, we began to talk about church planting, as well as look at other opportunities. I would like to say the path to church planting went without a hitch, but after four intense days of assessment, we were given a yellow light based primarily on the strength of our marriage. Because of our journey as a blended family, this did not come as a surprise, and for me at the time, it also came as a slight relief. However, as much as I know God's timing was right, this still brought up the repeated questioning of my value and ability to truly be in a place of leadership. Moments like these seemed to quickly bring to the surface my self doubt and a desire to simply count myself out again.

But, as God seems to have a way of doing, he placed us in a church where we were able to recover and heal in some areas that were much needed, whether we realized it at the time or not. This was a place where we learned to be more vulnerable in our leadership, created relationships that removed us from some of the ministry isolation we were living in, and continued to develop in us the gifts God had placed in us. It was here, as I watched other women lead and we watched other couples co-teach, that my husband and I learned how much we loved to communicate together. As I began to step out and develop in this new area of teaching with him (I may have had to invest this time in some great scarves instead of turtle necks), I began to feel more alive in this new arena than I had in a long time. My self-doubt would still creep in and does to this day, but I look back again at people who believed in me, who took the time to speak what they saw in me, and I know I would still be counting myself out were it not for them.

Today as my husband and I are almost one year into our church planting life (we finally got a green light!), we lead together. We believe this is one of the ways we can bring our greatest impact to this world. There is a lot more struggle between the lines of this story, but we do our best to stand tall in who God created us to be both individually and together when people question whether or not I should be in the role I am in. The opinions of others have shocked me at times, but I have decided to be done counting myself out or letting anyone else do the same. I have seen a faithful God who has whispered his words of love and belief to me every time I am tempted to doubt.

In closing, if you are a woman who struggles to see your leadership abilities or is tempted to listen to the voice of others, here are my words for you because of what God has been so committed to showing me:

1. Fight the battle of isolation like your life depends on it. Find women who have gone before you, who see what God sees in you, and who can stretch you—women who love Jesus more than they love you.

2. Be intentional to determine the lies that are on repeat or that sneak in at your most vulnerable moments. Every time they creep in, run to your heavenly Father, and ask him to show you the story only He can write with your life.

3. Push through the moments that stretch you and cause you to be uncomfortable—purchase turtleneck sweaters and scarves if you have to! These are the moments God will allow you to see what only he can do through you. Then and only then will you see your true identity come to life.

SECTION 4

SECURE IDENTITY

Named + Known

Securely Unfinished

Heidy Tandy

While I was a grad assistant working on my Master's at Illinois State, I was given the opportunity to have dinner at the University President's home. This was an annual tradition for orientation leaders during their rigorous training for one of the most sought-after leadership positions on campus. After a long day of coaching on how to give an effective campus tour (while walking backwards), we got all fancied up and headed to the President's house for a three-course meal that was surely one of the best we would have all year. We were given a crash-course on dinner etiquette that basically boiled down to: If you are certain you aren't going to like something, try it anyway.

Prior to this annual dinner, our names were submitted to the President's assistant so that we could each have professional name tags to wear when we got to the residence. As we were walking up to the door, we found a small table with the tags which were to be put on before sitting down for dinner. Despite my diligent search I couldn't seem to find mine. I knew they were planning on me. I had surely not forgotten to RSVP. Then, I saw it:

HIDI JO TRANDY, GRADUATE ASSISTANT

Well, at least they had my middle name right. I picked it up, tore off the backing, and stuck it on the lapel of my wrap dress to became Hidi Jo Trandy for the evening (and on multiple occasions throughout the summer). My fellow staff members and student leaders could not look at my name tag without laughing and neither could I! Each of the other twenty-five or more attendees were labeled perfectly, but somehow my name got a bit mixed up. Not exactly an identity crisis, more of a spelling snafu. I knew exactly who I was in spite of the mix-up, but that isn't always my story.

Does it feel as if everyone else knows who they are except for you?

Does secure identity feel like an elusive summit that you'll never reach?

When we first decided to plant a church in 2012, blogging was still incredibly popular, Facebook was in its prime, Pinterest was a new medium that everyone was talking about (especially women), and Instagram was rapidly becoming a place for people to creatively and beautifully document their lives. Unfortunately, I had unknowingly set myself up for failure because I was trying to make my life look just like the perfect images and stories I was hooked to online.

I was trying to make my home look flawless like a Pottery Barn catalog (on a Target budget), just like my favorite Instagram account.

I was trying to have a trim zero budget, pinching every penny, just like my favorite coupon clipper online.

I was trying to make all of my baby's food at home with the least amount of ingredients, just like all the mom chefs on Pinterest.

I was trying to keep my kid on a strict (but not too strict, because I'm a cool mom!) schedule, just like the other mommy-bloggers were doing. And whenever I googled anything about raising kids, I'd read how horrible of a mom I was—and how my kid would be scarred for life—for even thinking about putting my kid on a schedule.

I saw people on Facebook posting daily about how they were crushing P90X, and I could barely climb my stairs without getting winded.

I saw church planters who were less than one year old and crushing it with dozens of baptisms, crisp marketing, and full auditoriums.

I was completely overwhelmed with information and standards and pressure. So much pressure. One afternoon my husband Josh came home to eat lunch, and I began to give him all of my words before he even made himself a sandwich. Words turned to tears, and the tears turned to sobs.

Marriage tip: we have learned that sometimes I just have to get my words out. Sometimes this practice alone doesn't require anything from Josh; he can listen without solving, and it's a win for both of us. It's especially helpful for him to hear from the start that I don't need a solution. That frees him up to listen. This time was different: I needed help. And Josh knew it. In love, he gently told me, "You can't be all of those women all at once." That was exactly what I was trying to do.

This is why relationships are so important—whether it's a spouse, a close friend, or a mentor, we must have other voices in our lives who can help see our blind spots. Part of being secure in our identity is knowing that there are some things we cannot see on our own and being open to trusted voices in our lives.

I had created these requirements for myself that to me were non-negotiable, but to anyone outside of my head were completely unreasonable. Josh saw them while I just kept trying to perform to an unachievable standard.

Today I write this chapter being secure in the fact that I can't do it all. I sure try sometimes, striving to be super woman, super wife, super mom, super housekeeper, super chef, super volunteer, super employee, and super friend. This is a process that I am still not finished with. Yet I am okay being an unfinished product, even though I frequently have to be reminded to give myself grace by the people who know me the best.

So in this section, three women will share stories of victory: lessons about personality type, overcoming fears, and taking risks. It is my hope that we can all identify areas in our lives where we are living securely. Secure identity does not mean that we have all the answers or that we are in any way finished, but we're on our way to truly being ourselves.

This I Know For Sure

Kimberly Bolden

But now, this is what the Lord says—he who created you, Jacob, he who formed you, Israel:

"Do not fear, for I have redeemed you; I have summoned you by name; you are mine. When you pass through the waters, I will be with you; and when you pass through the rivers, they will not sweep over you. When you walk through the fire, you will not be burned; the flames will not set you ablaze. You are precious and honored in my sight, and because I love you."

Isaiah 43:1–4

When I was seven years old, I was challenged to a race by one of my classmates. The goal of this race was to be the first one to run across the schoolyard to the iron gate that marked the entrance of the school. This classmate taunted me about my inability to run fast enough and doubted whether I would win our race. She made it clear that though I may have been the teacher's favorite, I was not well liked among my peers and wanted to ensure that I did not forget it.

At the end of the race, I was shoved into the iron gate. Before I knew it, there was blood everywhere. My lips were swollen, and my tooth was broken—so sensitive to the touch that all I could handle was a bit of numbing gel from the side of the pinky finger. The pain was so severe that even the dentist recommended that the tooth needed to die before it was replaced.

This aggression and disdain by a childhood school bully influenced my narrative and made me completely self-conscious. I disliked posing for pictures, answering questions in class, and speaking in front of large crowds. My confidence quickly waned when individuals locked eyes with me trying to engage in conversation. I was honestly ashamed of my appearance.

Fast forward to seven years ago when God called us to plant a church. I distinctly remember navigating the CPAC (Church Planters Assessment Center) week with much reservation being sure not to speak out of turn or bring too much attention to myself. I wore my childhood pain as a badge of honor, secretly hoping that it would disqualify me from the call, yet it was at this assessment that I started to find my voice again. My team had just completed the worship service portion of the assessment, and I was asked by one of the assessors if I regularly spoke in worship gatherings, to which I replied with barely a whisper, "No." The assessor's response dually shocked me and stoked a fire in my belly. He said, "You should. Speak up! God has given you much to say. People will listen when you have something to say."

For so long, I believed that a broken tooth disqualified me from speaking truth. The deadliest of lies are the ones we often tell ourselves about ourselves. I started believing them because they were on repeat like a broken record. You know the lies. They are the ones that whisper we do not matter and that we are "just" women—the ones that shout that there is no greatness within us. These lies silence our voice. They clothe themselves in false humility spewing that our highest calling is solely wrapped up in one's call to marriage or motherhood. They tell you that you are too broken to be fixed.

Later that afternoon, I made a beeline for the mirror in our hotel bathroom. While standing facing my reflection in the mirror, I opened my mouth wide and bellowed. I was tired of being the victim in my own story. I stared at my reflection in the mirror and with a sense of purpose said, "Who told you that you were broken beyond repair? Who told you that you were naked? Who told you that your voice did not matter?" I had to look myself in the eye and speak truth to power. I reminded myself of God's promises.

For the last six years, I have used my voice to inspire and ignite God's people to action starting with myself. In the thick of church planting fires and the shower of church planting waters, I daily remind myself that I belong. God's call is not revoked based on my physical appearance or limitations. God exhibits his strength best in the center of my weakness. Because of Christ, I can lead strong.

I realized that everytime that I chose to speak up, people listened. When I raised my voice, people got quiet. It made me uncomfortable at first, but then I remembered that I was given a mantle to speak God's truth.

I had to reject the false narratives I chose to believe, whether it be the external narrative of what others said about me or the internal lies that I repeated to myself.

Success in church planting is faithfully using what you have where you are for the present season. God specializes in doing more with less. Do not ask for permission to live out the calling God has for your life. If we wait for the approval of people, we may never plant.

Remember you are chosen for this.

Reject the lies of false security and insecurity.

Recall God's promises.

Remind yourself that you are fully loved and fully known.

Raise your voice and speak up.

Remain humble.

Rest in God.

Repeat.

You are called. You are invited by the Creator of all things to reflect his glory in all areas of influence. Your obedience, not your giftedness, is God's highest delight. God will always do more with less. Know that every shortcoming, every sickness, and every closed door presents an opportunity for God to be glorified.

Rabid Extroversion

Katie Alesso

From the time I was a little girl, I knew I was a social butterfly. Like, a little neurotically so. I loved meeting new people, cherished big groups of friends, and thought parties were the coolest thing in the entire world. When I was eight, I remember poring over a little American Girl book called The Care and Keeping of Friends to discover any new gems about how to build relationships in a more effective way. Around the age of eleven, I coordinated a team of people to plan huge surprise parties for each of my parents' landmark birthdays. In college, I had a regular calendar of weekly dinners with friends and made sure that people knew they were a high priority in my life. As I understood myself then, God had hardwired me for friendship and gathering. But that's kind of where it ended—I loved becoming friends with people and hoped that it would somehow benefit their lives. I didn't understand the place friendship plays within the local church.

The idea of evangelism used to be so intimidating to me. I even went through a program when I was a teenager to learn how to share my faith, memorizing a specific outline with questions and transitions. But it actually made me more anxious. What if I get it wrong? What if I get off course? I knew who I was, but it didn't seem to match up with how I understood the church to work. Growing up in the church, I thought that there was one right way to do things: one correct way to share the gospel, one way to make disciples, one right way to commune with Jesus. I often didn't feel that I was doing the formula right. There was a call on my life from a young age, a longing to be part of what Jesus was doing in the lives of others. But I doubted that call because it didn't connect to who I was.

Jesus likes to use the most unexpected means to get my attention. A few years ago, we were considering church planting, but I still had a lot of questions and doubts. My husband, Andrew, and I always seem to have our best conversations in the car. One evening, after a long night of ministry, we sat in the driveway talking.

I clearly remember expressing, "I think church planting would involve opening our home and our family life in ways that I'm not sure I'm ready for. What would boundaries look like? What would God ask us to do? I'm not sure I'm ready to say 'yes' when I don't even understand what it would look like or what my piece would be in it." Here I was, someone who had always loved bringing people together, but taking on that responsibility in a church felt daunting to me.

Andrew said, "I don't know the answer to that, but let's pray about it together." We asked God to make it clear, and then we walked inside. About thirty minutes later (at 11:30 pm) we heard a knock on our door. Andrew answered, and a man we'd never seen said, "I've been wandering this neighborhood for hours tonight. God told me to knock on doors until I found a pastor to pray for me." It was late. We didn't know him at all.

Andrew said, "I'll come outside, and we can talk and pray." Inside, I made cups of hot cocoa for them because it was cold that evening. I was peeking through the blinds, praying, uncertain who this man was or what God was doing in the conversation. Andrew began praying with him, but he insisted, "No, your wife needs to come pray for me."

I didn't understand all of it yet, but I knew God was asking me to step into who he had created me to be. So I did the only thing I knew to do: I walked outside with those two cups of cocoa. Around midnight, as this man (who we later found out was a prostitute) kneeled to puke cocoa-tinged meth all over my front yard, I laid my hands on his shoulders and prayed for God to take away all the pain and darkness in his life and to give him newfound victory in Jesus.

That night, God spoke softly but distinctly to my heart that ministry is unpredictable, sometimes beyond my wildest dreams. I still wasn't one hundred percent sure about church planting, but I knew the job description included becoming a friend to hurting people, and that it was a lot less scary than I had anticipated. As I looked this man in the eye, there was nobody I'd rather be praying over that evening.

Jesus showed me that it's impossible to know everything he's calling me into before it happens. And even if I knew, it would overwhelm me. I simply needed to take the first step of faith, and he would provide what I needed for each moment. He would help me to build friendships with people who felt far from Jesus and help them find belonging and victory.

My experience in church had taught me that this was the kind of situation my husband was equipped for. But God had been asking me for years to do this. Interestingly, a man in the midst of an overdose knew I was ready to be his pastor before I did. God had to send a wild answer to prayer to grab my attention.

As I've begun the church planting journey, it has led me to ask the question, "How has God uniquely created me?" If the church is an elaborate impressionist painting of God meant to show his heart to the world, I'd like to think each and every one of us is a different shade of color used to paint his beauty. We each contribute a different little swatch of God's character, one bit of his heart and personality in a unique way to our circle of friends. I'm learning that I don't have to be the whole painting. Other people use their different hue to share the heart of Jesus with their world. I've discovered so much as I've asked what my hue is and considered the part it plays in the painting.

I've also realized that everyone's unique gifts just serve as a vehicle for the general mission that we are all called to. Everyone is called to evangelism. What does evangelism look like with your specific set of gifts?

Everyone is called to discipleship. What does it uniquely look like when you disciple others?

I'm wired for evangelism. It's just a different form of evangelism than I ever knew existed. Relational evangelism is the most natural approach for me, because I'm wired to make friends. When we first went through the church planter assessment process with Stadia, I realized God can actually use my rabid extroversion (that I've always tried to tame) to welcome people into his family. Woo came up as my top strength. Woo? What is woo? Well, woo is the ability to win someone over. Turns out, my somewhat obsessive desire to turn everyone I meet into a lifelong friend can be used for God's kingdom.

Remember how hesitant I was about opening our home and how concerned I was with boundaries? Well, we're a little over a year into our church plant, and now having people into our home is our favorite thing in the world. We just invited the whole church to brunch in our apartment over the holiday season, and my heart buzzed with joy for the rest of the day. It's funny thinking about how hesitant I was about that area of planting. Looking back, I see it's been one of our most joyful and fruitful areas of ministry.

Now I host movie nights, girls night out, and game marathons for all the random friends I make, inviting friends from our church along as well. My passion for forging friendships has ended up helping people find enough connection with new friends from the local church that now they're coming to church for the first time. Where I used to introduce people, I now couple introduction with invitation. I've seen that friendship finds its place in the church when we give people the gift of community within God's family and with God himself. I've become more secure in sharing my faith as I've learned my piece in that puzzle.

I'm grateful that God made me to be the quirky extrovert that I am. He has called me to serve his people, and that's an incredible honor. Who am I to question it? The fact that he has repeatedly pursued me to serve his people (even when I've asked 94,322 questions in the process) makes me all the more secure in my calling. If he can pursue me with that kind of love and grace, he can help me to pursue others in the same way.

From Rejection to Rest

Sarah Burnett

A number of years ago I was sitting on a pier in a little Ohio town called Lakeside. I was there to attend an annual retreat Bloom hosts for women in church planting. At this point, our church was four years old and growing rapidly, and many people were looking at my husband and me for advice on how to be successful in church planting. If they had been able to observe our lives for even a day, they would have seen what we believed the answer was: give, give, and give some more. Even though everything looked great on paper, internally I felt I could never do enough.

At the root of this insecurity was the lie that the health and growth of our church were dependent on me doing everything perfectly. I was the children's ministry director, helped with the planning and logistics of our outreach events, attended every church meeting, hosted a small group in our home, and planned playdates with moms in our church and our community. Our home was always open to anyone at any time, and there were frequently weeks where we had multiple people over everyday of the week. There were also two extended periods of time where we had people from our church living with us. Meanwhile, I was trying to be a good mom to three kids under four and a supportive wife to a husband who was working virtually all the time and who had reached the point of exhaustion.

Even with all that going on, I felt I wasn't measuring up to the job description of being a "good leader." It was almost as if the job description kept expanding, and every time I looked at it I found yet another thing, not realizing that I was the one who was writing it. To say I was busy is an understatement. I was completely overwhelmed and extremely tired. Yet I was plagued with questions like: Am I hanging out enough with everyone? Do people feel connected? Am I helping in all the ways that I possibly can? Am I doing enough? If I had done more, would they have stayed?

As the second day of the retreat rolled along, there was space for silence and solitude. The idea of stopping even for a half an hour to just be and to allow God to speak to me sounded great. Yet it was totally contrary to how I had been living my life. I was not used to it, so I attempted to imagine myself on a mountain top receiving wisdom and words from God. As I sat there on the pier, the talk from the previous night came to mind. The speaker focused on Exodus 3 and 4, when God calls Moses to lead the Israelites out of Egypt. Moses questions God's decision-making ability by telling God that he has the wrong guy. He should send someone else.[1]

I wrote in my journal: "I feel like you are calling me to lead leaders, and that scares the crap out of me." I questioned God about my leadership abilities, purpose, and identity. I wanted to be more effective and lead more people closer to God. I had all the right intentions and desires but lots of fear. My fear was that if I was bold in leading people, they would just reject me. Relating to Moses was not hard at all for me at this moment. Moses openly questions God about his own leadership abilities and what to do if he is rejected. God reassures Moses that he will be with him and later sends Aaron to help.[2]

As I traced those fears back in my mind, I realized they were from an old wound I was carrying. In college, I was really worried about my dad. It took

---

1   Exodus 3:10-11, Exodus 4:13.

2   Exodus 4:14-17.

me quite some time to work up the boldness to talk to him regarding concerns I was having about his health. I shared how much I loved him and wanted him to be around. Unfortunately in the end, he flat out rejected my concerns and said he was going to keep living the way he was living because it was his life. It was devastating at the time—the rejection so piercing.

Fast forward to that day on the pier: I felt that if I had the courage to lead leaders, I wouldn't be enough and would somehow be rejected, just like my dad did when I finally found the courage to be vulnerable with him. I ended that journal entry by asking God to help me overcome the lies and to help me be bold.

Over the next couple of months, I committed to evaluate everything I was doing and to figure out what God was asking me to do and not do anymore. Little did I know that my dad would suddenly pass away that winter. I got the call from my sister, and I was in shock. Everything slowed down. I couldn't keep going and keep functioning the way I had been.

I intentionally chose to enter a season of rest, stepping out of every role I had previously held. The only roles I kept were wife, mom, daughter, sister, friend, and part-time Bloom employee. When I felt like I couldn't carry my grief anymore, I received a phone call from a very close friend in church planting. She encouraged me to take care of myself. I rarely ever gave myself permission to rest. She gently reminded me that God's love did not depend on what I did or didn't do.

I felt I finally had the freedom to just rest in his love and to know that I didn't need to fear rejection or doing enough to please God. My worth and value as a child of God was already set. I didn't need to constantly adjust and readjust and do enough to measure up or be good enough.

In the quiet moments with God, he kindly revealed to me that my boldness and leadership in my dad's life was not just a moment of rejection. It was a moment that I led boldly and pointed him towards good and godly things. God taught me that I can do all the right things for all the right reasons, but in the end, I don't have any control over anyone else. It's so hard to learn surrender. I have learned that people have the right to make their own decisions, even when it affects the people that love them.

After six months of resting and waiting on God, I knew he was calling me to start something new at Revolution. I began to brainstorm about a new Welcome and Info team at Revolution: a group of people who understood that their their mission was to connect people to the church and assist them with their next steps. We created a one-stop shop where you could connect to groups, join serving teams, and ask questions.

I learned that people, even really intelligent people I had previously felt intimidated by, enjoyed following me, and I was good at making connections. This was an excellent step for me to stretch myself and realize that I can lead leaders. Starting out, I was very unsure of my identity as a leader. I worried people wouldn't want to join my team. In fact, some people I asked to join my team declined—and that was okay. I learned to handle disappointment and move on. I was able to see that in saying no to this new team, some people were actually making the necessary choice to take care of themselves. It did not mean that I was a terrible leader.

Becoming secure in my identity has meant becoming more and more okay with the fact that I am unfinished. I need to ask for help. People are going to say no, leave our church community, and disappoint me. But none of these things determines my value.

When my identity is based on becoming more and more of who God created me to be and less and less of who I think others want me to be, I become more and more secure. Security in my identity means living authentically and bringing my whole self to the people and situations to which I am called. It does not rely on constant production in hopes that I've done enough.

To stay secure in my God-given identity, I've learned that I need to take care of myself. Effective and healthy leaders take care of themselves. For starters, they admit when they need a break, schedule time to exercise, and make visits with a counselor a priority. Almost every amazing leader out there has a routine of self-care. I've learned that I am not at all effective when I am angry, hungry, lonely, or tired. I must take care of myself.

My journey towards a secure identity started with an inventory of my heart and later my gifts. I believe that times of quiet contemplation and rest are the starting place for where God speaks to us about our identity. God wants to use everyone to bring his kingdom here to earth and that is going to take the forceful will of men and women leading. It's going to take a secure identity in who I know God has called me to be and resting in his kind love for me and for everyone I interact with.

This first line may be familiar to you, but I resonate with the postures of surrender and courage the author encourages throughout the entire poem. There are many things we want to change that we cannot change. I pray that God would grant us wisdom to distinguish our calling and help us to surrender to his will.

> *God, give me grace to accept with serenity*
> *the things that cannot be changed,*
> *Courage to change the things*
> *which should be changed,*
> *and the Wisdom to distinguish*
> *the one from the other.*
>
> *Living one day at a time,*
> *Enjoying one moment at a time,*
> *Accepting hardship as a pathway to peace,*
> *Taking, as Jesus did,*
> *This sinful world as it is,*
> *Not as I would have it,*
> *Trusting that You will make all things right,*
> *If I surrender to Your will,*
> *So that I may be reasonably happy in this life,*
> *And supremely happy with You forever in the next.*
>
> *Amen.*[3]

---

3   Though debated, the "Serenity Prayer" is often attributed to Reinhold Niebuhr. It was made popular by Alcoholics Anonymous. (2001). Alcoholics Anonymous, 4th Edition. New York: A.A. World Services.

CONCLUSION

Fully Named + Known

Heidy Tandy

Attendance. Giving. Discipleship steps. Facebook traffic. Social events. Community connections. Leadership evangelism. Prayer requests. Marketing reach. These are just a few of the metrics that church planters track, with particular attention given to the prelaunch and first few years. Data matters and measurables count. But what about what you can't count? What about what you can't measure?

One metric not included on the list above is the amount of joking that happens within a launch team. It's a silly marker to think about, but I do think joking and having fun together can really support healthy team dynamics. Our own launch team at Movement Church began to hit its stride when they began to make fun of me. I'm not talking about mean-spirited humor or hurtful joking, but the kind that happens between people who have spent enough time together to notice one another's behaviors.

There's actually theory that supports these observations. In 1965, Bruce Tuckman penned the theory that small groups go through four different stages in their development: forming, storming, norming, and performing (a fifth stage of adjourning was added later).[1] Tuckman proposed that these stages are all necessary in order for a team to be the best that it can be: collaborating together to solve problems, navigating change, and working efficiently. Launch teams are no exception to these developmental stages.

In what Tuckman would argue would be the "norming" phase, our group started to notice something about me. Roughly six months into our church plant, our team began to joke that I had a phrase that I often repeated in our time together in the pre-service environment.

Have you ever stepped up to the pre-service meeting feeling like you've run a full marathon before the event even started? You think back to the previous three hours of set up and have a hard time thinking of anything that has gone to plan. You couldn't find the key to the lock on the trailer. The elementary school didn't have the heat on in January, delaying set up by an hour. Your lead vocalist came down with laryngitis (on a Sunday where you planned a stripped-down acoustic set because the rest of your worship team is out of town). You're out of chenille stems for your kids' ministry. And when you opened ProPresenter there was an email from a launch team friend telling you he had decided to go to another church. You step into the circle to pray and everyone is disheveled. You can feel it: the tension, defeat, and internal questioning of how the team was going pull off the worship gathering.

During these stressful pre-service meetings, no matter the circumstances, our team pointed out that I would frequently look at them and say, "It's going to be great." Sometimes I would say it nonchalantly; other times I would say it with determination, affirming that we were ready to go and the upcoming activity would indeed be great. I did not realize how much I said it prior to launching our church, but once someone pointed it out, I decided to keep using it. I needed to hear it just as much as our team did.

This has become a sort of mantra for our church. Most of the time it is referenced as an inside joke with our leaders, a side comment at the end of

---

1   Tuckman, B. W. (1965). Developmental sequence in small groups. Psychological Bulletin, 63(6), 384-399.

a meeting. My real-life people know that I think a good joke said with love and in love is my favorite. I adore that my friends pointed this out about me. The fact that I repeat "it's going to be great" is actually reflective of the kind of leader I want to be: a constant encourager who can do hard things.

Pointing out this behavior, however, has pushed me to reflect on my posture toward my identity. I want to look at my identity with a "it's going to be great" posture. I want to see myself the way Christ sees me. I want my inner dialogue to match my outside attitude. I believe the phrase "fake it 'til you make it" will eventually fail if there isn't a secure belief in your true identity. Sometimes I can pull off the "I have it all together" act like an Oscar-Winning Actress. But I have learned through experience and personal missteps that acting can only take you so far. It's exhausting.

The biggest lesson that I have learned in church planting is that sustainable growth and investment happens over time. It isn't a one-time event. It is consistently showing up to your own life and your own church. You don't just wake up one day and decide that you know who you are. It takes work. The work of delving into who we are, who Christ has uniquely gifted us to be is a process.

What if we consistently looked at our identity with this perspective of "it's going to be great?" This isn't overconfidence. This isn't denying the hard. Conversely, many of us daily navigate extremely difficult environments based on decades of social and racial inequity, warranted distrust in the church, and ultimately a broken world full of broken people. A perspective of "it's going to be great," however, means we know who we are and believe that every part of us is known and loved by God. With this belief firmly in place, regardless of our circumstances, we can move fearlessly forward empowered to maximize our roles in starting churches.

Why does this even matter?

I began to write something like: because our daughters our watching. Young women are watching. Watching how we will respond in this time and space where women are being given a louder voice and more opportunities for leadership advancement. And while I fully believe those things, I want to make it more personal. This matters because you matter. Your identity and your story matter in this generation because they matter to God. Not simply the larger story that he is writing for women, whom he has loved and elevated since the very beginning, but because you, [insert your name here], matter to him.

I encourage you to look back on these stories with intention: what resonated with you? What lies have you been believing that you need to throw out of your inner dialogue and vocabulary? What do you need to do to get one step closer to fully living in your Christ-given identity?

Maybe it's saying no to a bunch of small leadership opportunities to say yes to one big leadership opportunity.

Maybe it's embarking on a period of self discovery, where you educate yourself on yourself.

Maybe it's finding the courage to ask someone you respect what leadership gifts he or she sees in you.

Maybe it's taking that big risk you know you need to take.

Maybe it's simply saying, "God I'm not sure I can get through today. But I trust that you know me better than I could ever know myself, and I trust you."

Wherever you find yourself today on the journey of church planting, whether just dreaming, launching this year, or more than ten years in, I hope you can resonate with the stories of the women who have shared in this book.

Women who ask questions of God and believe what they hear, because they are Named + Known.

Women who push through hurt feelings and pursue forgiveness, because they are Named + Known.

Women who navigate unpredictable circumstances with grace, because they are Named + Known.

Women who seek the truth about who they really are in Christ, because they are Named + Known.

Women who, although unfinished, continue to bravely lead, because they are Named + Known.

May we pursue God's best for us and our churches as courageous and confident leaders, Named + Known.

It's going to be great.

EPILOGUE

We Need You

Greg Nettle

I grew up in a church where women could play the piano for worship, but they could not lead the congregational singing. Women could prepare communion, but they could not serve the elements. Females could teach males but only until the boys were in sixth grade (and supposedly became men). In many ways, it was a wonderful church, but it also had a strict code of what women could and could not do. The church shaped me, and it certainly shaped the girls who became women about their role in the local church.

When I went to Bible college, a very similar view of the roles of men and women was reinforced and anchored more deeply in my understanding of God's intent. All of my professors were male except for my piano instructor. We had chapel twice a week; never once was one of the speakers female. We (young men) were attending to become preachers, and the young women were attending to, umm, become good preachers' wives. In many ways it was a wonderful college, but it also had a strict code of what women could and could not do. The college shaped me, and it certainly shaped young women about their role in the local church.

Eventually, I became the Senior Pastor of a church in northern Ohio. I watched as women with obvious teaching gifts taught in our children's classrooms (very important but not fully utilized). I received counsel from talented women leaders who could speak into the direction of our church as long as it was outside of an Elders' meeting. I led worship when there were more capable females ready and willing to draw us into God's presence. I was perplexed. Why would God so obviously gift more than fifty percent of the members of our church and yet prohibit them from fully utilizing their gifting?

And so, our study began.

For seven years, our Elders (all men) wrestled with God's Word. We brought in theologians to speak with us—theologians who landed on both sides of the fence when it came to the biblical roles of men and women in the church. We prayed. We argued. We laughed, and we cried. Eventually, we concluded that God's desire for his church was that it be gift-based—not gender-based.

Many of you have similar stories. You, as women, have been raised in a church culture that limited the use of your gifting. Even though you are now in a setting that empowers you to fully become who God intends for you to be, you internally struggle to break free from your upbringing. Ladies, the church needs you!

We need you to be secure in your identity. We need you to fully understand and to identify with the journey on which God has placed you so that you can help lead others on their own journey. We need you to ground your identity in who God has created you to be so that you can fully express that identity in the life of the local church. We need you to serve with excellence, lead with humility and participate fully in helping the church become all that God intended her to be.

Many women and men have come a long way in our biblical understanding of our roles. Some of us are still on that journey of discovery. Women, regardless of where you currently land on the spectrum, be certain that our God who created you also knows you and has named you. He is calling you, and he is empowering you. He has created the beautiful body of Christ, the local church, to be your playground, your platform, and the love of your life. In the beginning, God created human beings in his own image. In the image of God he created them; male and female he created them.[1] So it was, and so it is intended to be.

---

1   Genesis 1:27 NLT.

ACKNOWLEDGEMENTS

I may be more excited to write this acknowledgements page than I was to write the book itself. As I am drafting this page, every chapter has been turned in, all the design work for the cover has been approved, and an incredible season (with a steep learning curve) of organizing this project is coming to a close. To say I feel grateful is an understatement.

Debbie Jones: you believed in this book and my ability to write and put it together before I did. Furthermore, you have consistently believed in me and my giftings way before I did. Your frequent phone calls where you push me to be confident are helping me to become the leader that I want to be. I am no longer faking it until I make it because of your relentless encouragement.

Dr. Tom Jones: your short visit to our team retreat last year at Lakeside helped to shape this book as well as our 2019 theme of identity. Thanks for making us better. And to the entire Stadia Team: thank you for celebrating this book and for unapologetically being a champion for women.

Vanessa Pugh: when I asked you to mentor me in 2015 and you said "I have time", I couldn't have asked for a better fit in someone to disciple me in this journey of church planting. Thanks for always pointing me to Jesus. You're one of my favorite Euchre partners.

To the writers that bravely shared their stories in this book—Kasey, Dimetra, Vanessa, Shannon, Jessica, Stacie, Sheila, Rachel, Michaell, Kim, Katie, and Sarah—thanks for saying yes. Thank you for pouring your energy into your chapters when clearly you are leading strong in several other arenas of your lives.

Dori Gorman: thank you for not blocking me on your phone. Thank you for answering my countless questions about everything from citations to layout to timeline, as well as your powerful prologue. Not only do you make me a better writer but your friendship draws me closer to Jesus.

Lisa Bennett: thanks for saying yes to story editing this book. You made this process so much smoother and exponentially more fun. I like working with you, and I respect you even more!

Meredith Camacho: your editing eyes have given me so much peace. And you may be one of the fastest email responders ever. Thank you for using your gifts to help maximize the excellence of this project.

Grace Johnson: I believe in you. I always have and always will. Your design eye is incredible, friend. What a privilege it has been to work with you.

Lena Roberson: thank you for working with Bloom again and laying out each of these stories with care. You made this process so simple!

Sarah Burnett and Becky Murphy: the 2019 theme as well as this book absolutely does not happen without both of your insights and perspectives. You also helped keep me focused this year and picked up extra tasks as I was head-down in finishing up this book. Can you believe we get to do this for our jobs?

To my community of women here in Northern Kentucky: you are amazing and encourage me to be authentic and real. As I began to list your names, I realize I could spend the entire acknowledgements section on you ladies alone. My relationships with you in NKY are the best surprise in church planting.

To the Movement Church community: almost five years in and I'm ready for more. You are our family here in Kentucky. I can't wait for what's next!

Mom and Dad: thanks for the extra grandkid sitting this past year, and for your extra encouragement as well, especially in times where you clearly see I'm trying to do too much. I know I drive you bananas. Yet, as family does, you keep showing up and loving our unique little family in the best ways. Remember when I wanted to be a Marine Biologist?

Grandma Connie and Papa Jim: thanks for doing the drive on 74 from Indy to Cincinnati, never knowing if you may take a kid or two home with you on the way back. Your support on our church planting journey has meant the world to us.

Jenny Mumaw: your friendship through many seasons of life and ministry is is one I will never take for granted. Jenny, I just want to be a good mom.

Isaac and Clara: you are my people and I am crazy about you. Isaac—you keep me laughing and growing. Clara--you are creative and brave and a leader at the age of 4. Being the C.O.O. of our spicy family never gets old.

Josh Tandy: I want to be married to you for no less than one hundred years. You are my favorite person. There's no one else I'd rather share a bowl of hot cheese with. Thank you for reading each section, for your careful and helpful feedback, and for helping me to translate my thoughts into chapters. I want to continue to lead and learn with you and can't believe we get to do this life together.

Jesus: you always know what you're doing. May I never take this journey for granted and always be fully welded to you.

CONTRIBUTORS

Dori Gorman

Dori Gorman and her husband, Rich, planted NewStory Church in Chicago, Illinois in January of 2011. They have been married for 12 years, and together they have been the Co-Lead Pastors of NewStory for the past nine years. Dori holds a Masters of Divinity degree from Emmanuel Christian Seminary, and she is gifted by God as a shepherd-prophet with a passion for preaching, coaching, discipleship, and coming alongside the forgotten. She is honored to partner with Stadia's Bloom ministry to help women maximize their role in starting churches. As a part of Bloom, she leads the Preaching Team and published a book, *Anonymous: Naming the God of Esther and the Women Who Plant Churches*. In her free time, Dori loves to read, rock climb, play basketball, and go on adventures with her family: Rich, Charis (7), and Nia (4).

Kasey Jane

Kasey Jane and her husband, Dave, planted Connect Church in Washington, Illinois in September of 2013. They have been married 21 years and have three amazing children: Benn (18), Will (16) and Emma (11). Kasey cares deeply for women and loves hearing their stories. You can often find her at her town's local coffee shop or out to lunch with a friend engaging in meaningful conversation. Family time is her most favorite, and she's currently trying to adjust to the idea of her firstborn leaving for college this fall.

Vanessa Bush

Vanessa Bush and her husband, Nate, planted New City Church in Albuquerque, New Mexico in 2010. Nate and Vanessa have have three kids: Micah, Corban, & Evangeline. When she is not chauffeuring children to soccer and ballet, Vanessa owns and operates Albuquerque Moms Blog, enjoys volunteering at church, loves watching college football, and drinks a little too much coffee. She is passionate about connecting women with each other, loving her people, and finding the good in her place.

Dimetra Barrios

Dimetra Barrios is co-lead pastor of Legacy Brooklyn with her husband, Richard. She is a Brooklyn native called to serve God in the very community she grew up in. She has studied at both Liberty University and Fuller Theological seminary. Most of her equipping apart from church and seminary comes from Redeemer City to City and Stadia. She has two amazing children: Lea (11) and Richard Jr. (9). Legacy Brooklyn will launch in the fall of 2019.

Shannon Smith

Shannon Smith and her husband, Dan, planted Momentum Christian Church in Cleveland, Ohio in 2005. Shannon is currently the Small Groups Director at Momentum. She also leads worship, hosts and leads a small group, and volunteers in the public schools. Shannon and Dan have been married 22 years and have three children: Zion (15), Azlan (14), and Journey (12). Shannon loves speaking to women of all ages and is passionate about loving God, loving people, and making disciples who make disciples (all while wearing her heels and drinking a cup of tea).

Jessica Moerman

Jessica and her husband, Chris, launched Grace Capital City in Washington, DC in September 2016. After several years of cross-hemisphere dating, Jessica and Chris married in 2008 and have one son, Liam (4). Passionate about understanding God's creation, Jessica has a Ph.D. in Earth and Atmospheric Sciences, researching how climate has changed throughout Earth's history. She is also passionate about seeking positive solutions to safeguard our communities and the next generation from the effects of a warming world. Jessica was recently featured on The Today Show for her work exploring the intersection of science and Christian faith.

Stacie Salva

Stacie Salva has partnered in ministry with her husband, Toney, for more than 25 years. Fifteen of those years have been spent as Children and Family Pastor at Discovery Christian Church, a church they planted near Pittsburgh, Pennsylvania. Stacie oversees a team of 100+ volunteers, but her proudest legacy are her two kids: Tanner (21) and Haley (17).

Sheila Brown

Sheila loves being on mission with her husband to win people for Jesus as well as getting people connected into community groups at their church. Her favorite job is being the mom to her three teenage daughters: Marissa, Makayla, and Myah. She loves playing games, sweet tea, her front porch swing, and meals shared together with friends and family around the table. Sheila and her husband, Jeremy, planted Journey Church in Jackson, Tennessee.

Rachel Short

Rachel Short is the Outreach and Connections Director at Project 938, a church that launched on Super Bowl Sunday, February 4, 2018, in West Chester, Pennsylvania. Prior to joining the Project 938 staff team, Rachel worked in the corporate world both in public relations and in fundraising consulting. Rachel is a graduate of the University of Texas at Austin, and she is currently pursuing a Master of Arts in Religion (MAR) at Westminster Theological Seminary. She is a proud Texan who believes God has called her to the East Coast to connect people to the person and mission of Jesus through the people of Jesus.

Michaell Dupin

Michaell Dupin has been a leader in the local church for the past 18 years. She is passionate about coaching, equipping, and training leaders. She and her husband, Clint, recently planted Eastown Church in the San Francisco Bay Area with a focus on loving their community and connecting people to the adventure of following Jesus. Michaell is also a talented teacher, often preaching at the weekend services of Eastown. She has found her voice and calling as a woman and leader in the local church and works hard to help other women do the same to make an impact in their communities, families, and places of influence. Michaell and Clint have four children ranging in ages from six to 24 years old; there is a lot of activity, laughter, and adventure in their home.

Kimberly Bolden

Kimberly Bolden is the Communications Director for Peachtree Christian Church in midtown Atlanta. She and her husband, Wesley, successfully planted Tri-Cities Church in Atlanta, Georgia in 2013. Kimberly is passionate about equipping women for effective service and leadership in the church and enjoys travel adventures, photography, and a great cup of chai.

Katie Alesso

Katie Alesso lives in Los Angeles with her husband, Andrew, and their two-year-old son, Dax. Katie is the Connections Pastor at Thrive LA Church, which she and Andrew planted in September 2017. They really enjoy the diversity, vibrant food scene, and artistic heartbeat of LA. Katie previously worked as an elementary teacher and holds her Masters in Curriculum and Instruction. She loves ice cream, audiobooks, and seeing people find meaningful community with Jesus and with one other.

Sarah Burnett

Sarah Burnett is an energetic and passionate leader who loves to empower people to reach their potential in church planting. Sarah has been a part of growing and developing the Bloom ministry for the last nine years and currently leads in Stadia as the Associate Director of Communications for Bloom. She hosts the Plant Strong Podcast, a podcast that empowers women to maximize their role in starting churches. She was as contributing writer for Bloom Where You're Planted: Vol. 2 and Anonymous - Naming the God of Esther and the Women Who Plant Churches. In partnership with Stadia and Orchard Group, she and her husband Josh planted Revolution Annapolis in Maryland in 2010. Together they have three children: Savannah, Grady, and Madelyn.

Greg Nettle, Stadia President

Greg Nettle has a God-given passion for The Church and its responsibility to plant new churches—churches specifically designed to reach out to children at physical and spiritual risk. He is an author, speaker, and consultant as an agent of change in the global church. For 25 years, Greg served as visionary leader of the RiverTree Movement in Ohio. During that time, the church grew from

100 to more than 3,000 people, from one to four campuses, helped plant 15 churches throughout Ohio and 13 in Latin America, sponsored more than 2,000 children with Compassion International, and involved more than 200 families in adoption. Greg came to RiverTree after beginning his ministry as a church planter in Dublin, Ireland. Greg's sense of adventure has taken him around the world as he has climbed Mount Kilimanjaro, Cotopaxi, and Whitney among others to raise funds to bless children on the margins of society. Greg's most important partner in life is his wife, Julie, as they lead their children, Tabitha and Elijah, to fall deeply in love with Jesus. Greg has co-authored three books: Small Matters in collaboration with Compassion International President Jimmy Mellado, One Of, and Disciples Who Make Disciples.

ABOUT THE EDITOR

Heidy Tandy, Editor

Heidy Tandy serves as the Associate Director for Bloom and is passionate about helping women thrive in church planting. Bloom is a ministry of Stadia, an organization that plants churches that intentionally care for children. She and her husband, Josh, planted Movement Church in Newport, Kentucky in March of 2014. They have been married for 13 years and have two kiddos, Isaac (6) and Clara Jo (4), who keep her laughing and on her toes. A graduate of Anderson University (BA, 2005) and Illinois State University (M.Ed, 2009), Heidy's professional background in Higher Education and Student Development has greatly informed her work both in and outside of the local church. Heidy prefers a mountain vacation over a beach vacation, tacos over sushi, and a Sunday afternoon watching football with her people over most any other activity.

YOUR
CHURCH
PLANTING
EXPERTS

Learn more at StadiaChurchPlanting.org.

DON'T PLANT ALONE

bloom
CHURCH PLANTING WOMEN

Join Bloom now at StadiaBloom.com.